Viral politics

Viral politics

communication
in the new media era

edited by **Anthony Painter**
and **Ben Wardle**

Politico's
PUBLISHING

First published in Great Britain 2001
by Politico's Publishing
8 Artillery Row
Westminster
London
SW1P 1RZ

www.politicos.co.uk/publishing

Copyright © Anthony Painter and Ben Wardle 2001

The right of Anthony Painter and Ben Wardle to be identified as the authors of this work has been asserted by them in accordance with the Copyright, Designs & Patents Act, 1988.

A catalogue record of this book is available from the British Library.

ISBN 1 84275 022 4

Printed and bound in Great Britain by Bell and Bain

All rights reserved. No part of this publication may be reproduced or transmitted in any form or by any means, electronic or mechanical including photocopying, recording or information storage or retrieval system, without the prior permission in writing of the publishers.

This book is sold subject to the condition that it shall not by way of trade or otherwise be lent, resold, hired out, or otherwise circulated without the publishers' prior consent in writing in any form of binding or cover other than that in which it is published and without a similar condition being imposed on the subsequent purchaser.

Contents

	Introduction	vii
1	The contagious campaign • (part 1) • *Anthony Painter*	1
2	Measuring digital campaigns • *Mike Bloxham and Andy Meyer*	49
3	How e-democracy can help deliver better public services • *Stephan Shakespeare*	72
4	Unified message, many channels • *Ben Wardle*	93
5	The new political machine • *Chris Casey*	117
6	Labour: the e-campaign is born • *Kate McCarthy and Andrew Saxton*	129
7	E-campaigning: active and interactive • *Justin Jackson*	142
8	The contagious campaign • (part 2) • *Anthony Painter*	154
	Notes on contributors	169

Introduction

Anthony Painter and Ben Wardle

➥ We live in strange political times. In the past year, the fuel distribution system has been brought to a grinding halt, a conflagration of racially motivated riots has swept towns in northern England, wrongfully identified paedophiles have been burnt out of their homes, anti-globalisation/capitalism riots have resulted in hundreds of injuries, arrests and a death, a leading politician had a brawl with a protestor in full view of the TV cameras.

And yet, the Labour Party romped home with a landslide majority barely diminished from the previous election. We are more prosperous than we have ever been, unemployment is low, the British inflationary disease seems to be dormant, and billions of pounds of public investment is just starting to arrive in the budgets of local managers.

On the one hand we've never had it so good, on the other we are frustrated, enraged and patronised.

The main story that emerged from the British general election of 2001 was not the size of Labour's majority. It was the staggeringly low turnout – the lowest since an out of date wartime electoral register meant an exceedingly low turnout in 1918. It seems that while a few are choosing to hurl abuse, bricks, and punches, most are choosing to simply aim a well-targeted cold shoulder at the political system. Government claims contentment explains the electorate's conspiracy of silence. Only one positive approval rating for the government in the past year (and this was after the election) suggests that something rather less transient is occurring.

This context, a context of disengagement, is the starting point for *Viral Politics*. The contributors come from different professional worlds, different perspectives, and different sides of the political fence. One thing binds them all. They see that the environment in which politics exists is changing and they passionately believe that politics and government have to change to fit this environment. Another common factor for all the contributors is that they are the people who are engaging intellectually and practically with the challenges and opportunities presented by new technology and media. They are not only observers, they are the practitioners.

Politics and business find themselves in a new environment. The old communications tools – traditional PR and lobbying – are not nearly so effective. Information is profuse, the 'message' is increasingly common rather than private property, and individuals are far more likely to engage as a condition rather than as duty. Welcome to the new media era.

The new media era is often played out in the symphony hall of mass media but it is orchestrated in a different fashion. Technology is merely the infrastructure of the new media era. It is the people who are its presenters, directors and participants. It is a communications environment where culture has shifted and expectations have increased. It is an environment to which politics has yet to adapt.

So why did we decide to call this collection *Viral Politics*? It is the nature of a virus that it requires a host to incubate it and spread it. That's how it thrives. It must be so in the era of new media. New media is characterised by fragments and flickers accessed through multiple channels. For a virus to thrive in this uncertain, conditional and user-empowered environment, it needs hosts. The problem that you have in politics is that if your 'messages' – the language, symbols, and celebrities of your political narrative – kill off their hosts then your messages will just rattle around the hollow tin that is the 'Westminster Village'.

Quite simply, if politics doesn't re-learn how to aim its messages at new generations with wholly different expectations, then it will become increasingly disengaged. The contributors consider a whole range of challenges: how the electorate can be made into stakeholders, how politics can go about the business of recreating a language that connects rather than alienates, how politics has started to adapt, the difficulties that business is also having in managing its issues with the rise of 'citizen-consumers', and what technologies will come to dominate in the near future. We don't claim to have all the answers but we hope that *Viral Politics* has started to ask some of the right questions.

What is clear is that the context of politics has changed but this is something that politicians have only just realised. The fate of one party or viewpoint is not what is at stake. The challenge is to maintain and improve democracy and public service. Hopefully, it will be a matter of 'needs must', not 'you can't teach an old dog new tricks'.

Politics has to engage, interest, challenge and mobilise support. It has to accept the new media environment as no longer science fiction. New media is more about culture than technology. And modern culture is gradually making itself immune to conventional politics. Politics has to find a place for itself in a frenetic modern world. If politics fails, there is risk that it will find no space at all.

0.1 • Contents

➡ In *The Contagious Campaign (part 1): Politics in the era of new media*, Anthony Painter elaborates on the core thesis outlined already in this introduction.

From policy prescriptions for reconnecting the electorate we move onto measuring the success (or otherwise) of such ideas in practice. Mike Bloxham, CEO of digital research specialist Netpoll, and his colleague Andy Mayer outline a clear methodology in their chapter *Measuring Digital Campaigns*.

With the bursting of the net bubble, the 'old' rules of commerce and communication have been brought back into play. Bloxham and Mayer argue that robust planning and evaluation should form a key component of any attempt by political parties to engage with voters through new communication channels. They say that in their user surveys they have found that the feeling of user control gained through interrogating and cross-checking information is always cited as one of the principle benefits of the use of interactive media.

As involvement is the single most important factor in influencing communication online, they believe that without involvement there can be no communication. The chapter then goes on to explore the use of a 'scorecard approach' to develop a research methodology around which political campaigns can be developed, measured and adapted. Their scorecard forms a basis by which off-line as well as online campaigns can be measured.

The interactive nature of new media is not just a boon for political campaigning. As Stefan Shakespeare, co-founder of online polling and e-consultation company Yougov.com, describes in his piece *How e-democracy can help deliver better public services,* how new technologies can be used to empower citizens and consumers. Shakespeare believes that successive British governments have been suspicious of tools such as referenda, and have instead resorted to opinion polling and focus groups in an attempt to gauge satisfaction with and likely reaction to different policies.

The chapter conjectures that the introduction of stakeholder consultation was a worthwhile move, but that modern citizens don't have the time or inclination to attend turgid public meetings or take part in bureaucratic processes that may be hijacked by interest groups.

Shakespeare goes on to compare the legitimacy of internet polling with more traditional methods involving phone, face-to-face or self-completion of questionnaires. He believes that sampling difficulties will fade away as use of the net grows, but that internet polling offers key advantages in terms of speed, the use of audio and video, and the creation of panel-based polling to track niche opinion changes.

The ability to easily conduct follow-up surveys and facilitate 'negotiated solutions' is seen as one of the strongest reasons for using the internet in a consultation process in a way that is far more complex than using traditional methods.

Shakespeare outlines who he feels will benefit from the process stating "citizens are more likely to understand the difficult choices being faced; they are more likely to get their needs addressed, in the context of what is realistic. Government can be more confident in its actions; it can truly say it is serving the people, not exploiting them for power." He also argues that the corporate world would benefit from similar techniques and be seen as closer and more responsive to their customers' preferences and values (something which Anthony Painter comes back to in his closing chapter).

Ben Wardle opens *Unified Message, Many Channels* with a dystopian vision of a politics run by an all-powerful machine with populist tendencies. The chapter goes on to discuss how technology can be used to integrate the many strands of contact that parties have with the electorate.

Wardle argues that political parties must adapt and adopt the techniques of targeting and personalisation that are common to the best e-commerce sites. Content should be tailored to meet the needs of specific interest groups using data collected from a variety of sources. Data protection and privacy policies must however be transparent and robust to avoid accusations of Orwellian behaviour. A new breed of political 'data mining' experts will need to sit alongside the existing armies of pollsters.

He also discusses the relative merits of new communication channels such as digital television and third generation (3G) mobile phones. In the light of warnings of poor performance from future 3G operators the healthy scepticism in the chapter seems particularly apt. The piece outlines the likely changes in technology and take-up in the European mobile communication market and concludes that text messaging (of the old fashioned and rich multimedia varieties) will become increasingly important for voter communication.

Finally he argues the case for the use of collaborative Open Source software for the rapid development of robust and cost effective online political solutions.

Chris Casey, who has worked on e-campaigns for the likes of Al Gore, Hilary Clinton and Ted Kennedy, puts the internet in an historical context with his chapter *The New Political Machine*. Weaving together Thomas Jefferson with US government IT officials, Casey constructs an intriguing narrative around the development of the internet and its use by government, parties and voters. He takes the idea of the Tammany Hall style political machine of old (smoke-filled rooms and dirty deals) and brings it forward to the 21st century, dubbing campaigning on the net as the 'New Political Machine'. Only unlike Tammany Hall, the New Political Machine can be a far more empowering and inclusive engine for change.

The internet's growth as a key information and interactivity channel in the US is outlined with demographic data to highlight its importance as a campaign medium.

The next two chapters come from the hearts of Millbank and Smith Square. *Labour: the e-campaign is born* is penned by Kate McCarthy and Andrew Saxton of the Labour Party, while Politico's Design MD and former Tory webmaster Justin Jackson gives us *E-campaigning: active and interactive.*

Both pieces take us on a whistle-stop tour of how two old political machines made use of the New Political Machine in the 2001 General Election. The chapters discuss how the Labour and Conservative parties used new media to meet the needs of a variety of audiences in a 'timely, responsive and interactive fashion', mobilising supporters, raising funds and providing comprehensive information for floating voters and journalists. They also describe how the party net campaigns were used as stories in themselves to gain media coverage.

The party websites were the main communication tool, but regular e-mails to tens of thousands of supporters were a key means of getting information out quickly to those on the ground. Labour made extensive use of text messaging in the final week of the campaign, sending a series of messages to an opt-in list.

Justin Jackson makes the point that campaigning on the internet should always take its lead from the existing political campaign framework, but the trick is to shape the messages to meet the needs of a very different communication medium.

Anthony Painter revisits the Contagious Campaign in the final chapter of the book, *Business in the New Media Era*. He argues that in the era of mass media, business and politics used remarkably similar tools – centring on the contact book and the boozy lunch. But in the new media age businesses, like political parties, must come to terms with the fact that it is now harder and more costly to manage your public image.

A more cynical public, diffuse communication channels and well organised competitors and interest groups are all big challenges. Company behaviour is far more of a factor in people's purchasing decisions than ever before. Not just the ethical consumer, but also the new, young, middle class 'brand generation'. Painter goes on to review the case studies of Esso, Shell and Monsanto – from which all business can draw a number of lessons.

One shouldn't usually reveal whodunit, but to give away the ending of the book: "the future will belong to businesses who accept that the values embodied by their brand are now shared and cannot be controlled. Control is temporary, shared ownership is forever. The old outlets, contacts and methods are ceasing to be effective. A number of companies have led the way but will others have the courage to follow?"

And that is, ultimately, the message of the book. The cultural landscape has changed. Popular consciousness has changed with it. And that will be the central challenge for politics and business over the next decade – to adapt or allow others to adapt before you.

1.

The contagious campaign • (part 1)
Politics in the era of new media
Anthony Painter

1.0 • Introduction • the twilight of the mass media age

Political systems are engulfed in a structural crisis of legitimacy, periodically wrecked by scandals, essentially dependent on media coverage and personalised leadership, and increasingly isolated from the citizenry.

[*The Rise of the Network Society*, Manuel Castells][1]

➡ Politics needs a home. The cultural environment is shifting from the mass media age to the era of new media. Politics, its personalities, its organisation, its language, and its core assumptions remain firmly situated in the mass media age. Citizens feel dislocated from politics. The core challenge of today's politics is to find a language, set of symbols, and celebrity that can reconnect with citizens whose primary cultural experiences are through new media. In other words, politics has to adapt to the era of new media.

The movement of collective space away from legislatures, city halls and meetings in dusty village halls dominated by the theatrical orators happened long ago. From the beginning of the last century, politics moved from a charmed period of face-to-face politics to a collective space dominated by the mass media.

Politicians were slightly slow on the uptake. Print media came to dominate politics and the politicians eventually caught on. By the late 1950s, television was as pervasive a medium as print and politicians started to realise this by the late 1960s. However, it wasn't until the late 1970s that politicians started to perfect the arts of operating in an era of billboard advertising, the broadcaster-commentator, and partisan press. The era of mass media had achieved its apotheosis. Politicians did catch up eventually but it took a while.

When the world's biggest companies pledge their future to the construction of a service-based, entertainment enriched, global communications infrastructure that is the new media, it is time to take note. Entertainment and communications giants are waltzing together in increasingly perfect time. The merger of AOL and Time Warner is merely a symptom of the new environment.

Telecommunications, the entertainment industries – the cultural producers of the modern age – are becoming an inextricable whole, unified in the desire to forge a new collective space in their commercial and brand image.

So where is this new collective space to be found? This question strikes at the heart of the issue of why politics may be entering a period in which it will be increasingly difficult for politicians to achieve legitimacy for executive action. Politics is already becoming victim to a series of direct and violent attacks which it is all too easy to dismiss as the actions of extremists. The conspiracy of direct action is nothing in comparison with the conspiracy of silence exhibited by the electorate – notably, a *majority* of the young electorate.

The contention of this chapter is that our collective space – where we are entertained, discuss issues outside of the personal, act on and consider political issues – has changed, and that these changes have profound consequences for politics. Entertainment, communication and the economy have already felt the force of these changes as corporate networks form and dismantle. The creative and entertainment space becomes global, and access to diversified communications media becomes the badge of citizenship. *Our collective space can be accurately described as 'new media' rather than mass media.*

The new media environment is something more profound, involved and all-encompassing than mass media was. It cuts across numerous delivery 'channels': terrestrial television, digital television, satellite television, mobile phones, PDAs, the internet, broadband internet. It is accessed by many devices and used in many ways. It is collective space where diversified symbols and meanings are shaped and responded to in the self-image of the participant. The attention span of the participant in any fragment of digitised information is small but the search for the latest experience, even if only momentary, is profound. Celebrity is the ideal and involvement is the principle. The new media world is a world of flickers, fragments, and the latest kick.

1.1.1 • Identifying new media

There has been so much discussion over the past few years about the new economy, e-commerce, e-business, peer-to-peer trading, the new services, networking, the digital divide and any number of new technologies and wacky business models. For all these questions, statistics about access, profits warnings and exuberant investment decisions, an important shift has been obscured. More and more people (and, to conjecture, the majority of those aged under 30) are expressing their identity through the new media. New media, and the particular culture that is defined through it, is rapidly becoming an accurate metaphor for society.

The vast majority of young people engage in one or more of using a mobile phone, watching digital television, or accessing the internet in some environment. It is not fad. It is the cultural and psychological disposition through which they are defined.

The internet, web-sites, mobile phones and e-mail are just mere access points for the cultural and social phenomena that is the 'new media'.

A symbol of the new media is, of course, *Big Brother*. Much comment has been made about the fact that 16 million people voted in *Big Brother* (26 per cent of the votes were placed on the interactive TV platform) – significantly more than the number of people who voted for the Labour Party in the 2001 General Election. That simple fact is interesting enough but a look at the *Big Brother* phenomenon itself is even more intriguing and reveals a great deal about the new media.

Here we have eight ordinary people who are plucked from their everyday life and incarcerated in a prefab house in the East End of London for nine weeks. Notice that the programme is, in the first place, experienced on Channel Four – a conventional terrestrial channel. But then you have to add the multi-media web-site, the 200,000 people who signed up for mobile alerts, the hype, PR and advertising, and the always-on cameras on a digital channel. Still we have not adequately described the Big Brother phenomenon. There are the furtive e-mails at work, the mobile conversations and text-messages, the debates down the pub and the bets placed on the winner, and we are now starting to gauge what new media means and why Big Brother is one of the phenomena at the very apex of the concept.

The new media builds dramatic narratives around the mundane, takes the ordinary and creates celebrity, turns passive viewers into participants and constructs the life meaning out of entertainment. With new media, you are not an observer, but to part of the story. That is the real socio-cultural meaning of new media as epitomised by Big Brother.

New media has managed to embed itself within society in a very short space of time. In the early part of the new millennium, before 'new media' (diverse entertainment, user-participation, and global communications combined) constitutes the predominant cultural and collective space of our society.

1.1.2 • Politics in another time, another place

In the political sphere, there has been much debate about the efficacy of e-campaigning. For the purposes of discussion, we will define e-campaigning as marketing strategies of political parties and organisations aimed at issues management through the internet. This question is a mere fragment of something more fundamental. Does politics operate and function in a way that is adapted to the new collective space – the new media?

It is difficult to find incontrovertible evidence that we are experiencing a 'structural crisis of politics' as postulated by Castells in the opening quote. A 'structural crisis' would mean that politics would be unable to cope with the problems set for itself, and by the socio-economic environment, without undermining its own legitimacy. We have not returned to the international political and economic instability and political impotence of the 1970s, yet this should not induce complacency.

There are three circumstances in the current political environment that should caution against any complacency:

- The majority of young people and significant minorities of other groups inhabit a collective space better typified as 'new' rather than mass media. This group is continually increasing in size.
- People are no less interested in general political issues than they were a decade ago.[2]
- There is growing evidence of increasing alienation from conventional and traditional political institutions particularly amongst the young. Turnouts are down, more people are voting on local or protest issues and parties, politicians are no longer trusted.

In this environment, the electorate, and especially the young, are increasingly disengaged from conventional politics despite being no less interested in general political issues than they were a decade ago.

Simply put, politics is not connecting. It is not connecting because political organisations and personalities have not yet appreciated the scale of cultural change with which they are contending. They operate in the era of the mass media. In that era, 40 or 50 contacts in the mass media were sufficient, your opposition was well defined, and you knew that if your message was communicated effectively through the evening news you'd had a good day.

The mass media world is made for the little black books of spin doctors, off-the-record briefings, long lunches fuelled by fine wine and the message as medium. It is a world which seems to be thriving and well to its participants.

To the rest of us, it is a world in which political discourse is starting to sound hollow. Increasingly introspective and irrelevant narratives replace the image of the brilliant advertising machine that was the Conservative Party during the 1980s and early 1990s and the new Labour media machine of the mid-1990s. News becomes personal and gossip fuelled. Brown versus Blair, Portillo versus Hague, who is for whom and who can't work with whom, become the meta-narratives of a media increasingly bored by the intricacies of policy and delivery. Genuine political conflict and competition become diminished and distilled into gossip and personality. There is an appearance of consensus whatever the reality.

It is a vicious circle. Politics is spoken in inaccessible language, characterised by insipid messages aimed at media manipulation. In response, the media looks to create celebrity in politics like much of the modern media does in other areas. The only problem is that your average politician doesn't really appear to have many of the media-friendly skills that really constitute modern celebrity. Give me Robbie Williams over Michael Portillo anytime. Therefore, the mass media presentation of politics becomes a mixture of the anodyne and ridiculous.

The tragedy of this developing state of affairs is that politics is now just a fragment, a virtual reality, an experience to plug into for the latest kick. A functional democracy is just as important now as it always has been – to counter-balance and to provide a basis for private action. Politics matters but the media-political complex makes it seem unimportant.

This argument started with a pessimistic prophecy. It should end on a note of optimism. Politics, politicians, the public, and political parties have always managed to adapt to new environments previously: universal suffrage, economic crisis, new political causes and challenges. They can adapt again. In fact, political parties and government have already started to adapt, but only just. The right questions have to be asked in order to appreciate the cultural change that politics is facing.

The challenge is not one of technology. Technology and culture are inextricably linked. The issue is not whether e-campaigning works but does politics now exist in a new cultural landscape? If yes, and the basis of this argument is that it does, then should politics respond and if so how?

Optimistically, politicians can challenge the language, jargon, control, and cosy media-political relationships that characterise the era of the mass media. In replacement, they have to develop a set of personalised, open, and relevant messages that, while 'on message', appreciate that this can be a far more subtle concept in era of new media. Message becomes far more targeted – message in context as medium rather than simply message as medium.

In order for governments to maintain legitimacy and govern with authority it is necessary for politics to replenish itself from time to time. A process of replenishment is now necessary. Politics can stay just as it is but alienation will increase, direct action will be mobilised and corporations will start to view politics as an irrelevant irritation. In a few years we could be wishing that we could go back to the days when turnout was 59 per cent. The challenge is clear but will politics respond?

1.2 • The alienated many: a disconnected politics

➡ Nothing can be so simply observed as the complexity of the modern world. Just a couple of decades ago politics could be reduced to bi-polar realities of East versus West, socialism versus capitalism, tax versus public spending, business versus unions, inflation versus unemployment, and many other 'truths' arrived at by sleight of a reductionist hand. Complexity does not mean that political conflict is over or there's no left or right. It does mean that documenting and understanding political change is a little more tricky.

Our central aim is to look at the phenomenon of a citizenship disengaging from the formal institutions of democratic politics. There are multiple analyses of the problem but when you place them side by side they do not seem to amount to a convincing analysis of change.

Within the space of a decade, the British political class has changed from being trusted by the electorate, around 75 per cent of whom would vote, and were more actively engaged in politics, to having a political class that is not trusted or even liked by the electorate, who increasingly fail to vote.

Democratic systems depend on replenishment if they are to thrive. New voters must be imbued with a sense of civic engagement and active responsibility if governments are to assemble the popular resources necessary to face complex problems. What is clear from analysing voter trends in the 2001 election, quite apart from turnout being the lowest since 1918, is that politics is not even engaging a majority of the youngest voters. If circumstances remain the same then democratic participation is in severe jeopardy of not being replenished.

From the perspective of analysing the shift of mass to 'new' media, this is a salient point. The generation who most readily exhibit the consciousness, preferences and commitments of a new media environment is the very same generation that is disengaging from politics. The consequences of this state of affairs, if left unattended, will be to further worsen the sense of dislocation of the people from politics.

Undoubtedly, there are many different causes of low turnout. Since the 2001 British General Election, many explanations have been advanced to explain low turnout. These explanations fall into four categories:

1 *circumstantial* • 'the people were contented to see a second Labour government'
2 *institutional* • 'if it was easier for people to vote, or we had Proportional Representation or more local democracy then people would be more engaged'
3 *the end of politics*[3] • 'government has surrendered the public realm to corporations and the global economy renders government powerless so people don't think that it's worthwhile to vote. Parties are all the same which perpetuates the problem'
4 *media-political complex* • 'politicians and the media are increasingly talking to one another in a language and with a set of priorities that is impenetrable to the electorate'.

These theories are analysed in more depth below. But first, it is necessary to look at the actual phenomenon of increasing public disengagement from conventional politics itself.

1.2.1 • The features of alienation

Low turnout is not a bad thing in itself. It is the underlying process that it signifies which may be a cause for concern. It can be quite a rational and reasonable judgement (though maybe a little risky) that (i) your vote won't change an outcome that you may or may not be contented with, (ii) that the set of institutions in which you are participating does not really have a great deal of power to change your life (explaining, for example, low turnouts in local elections).

However, when taken as a whole, it seems that more fundamental processes were at play in the General Election of 2001. When polling and focus group data from the election period is analysed, it is clear that there is a dislocation between people's expectations of the political system and the capacity for delivery that it is perceived to have.

Six features characterised voting in the General Election:

1. *Low overall turnout* • Turnout dipped to its lowest level since 1918 with only 59.4 per cent of the electorate voting – just 26.4 million of a potential 44.5 million votes. There was no significant difference between England, Northern Ireland, Wales and Scotland.

    The low turnout in this election follows the lowest turnout since the war in 1997 (71.4 per cent) and constitutes a sharp fall on this figure. It also follows a turnout of 24 per cent in the 1999 European elections (down 12.5 per cent on 1994: Electoral Commission (2001, 12)). There has been no significant decline in how important politics is to people throughout the 1990s.

2. *Low turnout amongst the young* • MORI estimates that turnout amongst 18–24 year-olds was only 39 per cent. The same report found that attitudes to voting are no different between this group and other groups – they are just as likely to see voting as something which is important and can make a difference. Only 15 per cent claimed to have 'no interest in politics' as a reason not to vote.[4]

This group was the second most likely to watch party election broadcasts and see political billboard adverts.[5]

When you take into account general attitudes to politics and interest levels, it is difficult to characterise this group as being apathetic. In fact, they are a relatively engaged group when it comes to politics as a whole. They just seem to feel short-changed when it come to the *actual* operation of politics currently.

3 *Media interest/coverage* • Throughout the election the broadcast media was focused on 'election process' between 40 per cent and 60 per cent of the time according to research completed by the Communications Research Centre at Loughborough. Coverage was presidentialised (for example, Tony Blair appeared in 35.4 per cent of all election news items). The issue of most interest was Europe which featured in 9.5 per cent of news items (note that Europe is not the issue of highest concern to most voters).

The dearth of quality policy analysis is displayed in the reaction of voters to the news. While audiences for the BBC's *Ten O'Clock News* were up by 8 per cent on 1997, the comparable figure for the ITN news was down by 24 per cent constituting a significant net reduction (total viewing figures for the two channels were roughly similar). Viewers of the ITN news were actually *down* on the pre-election period with the BBC news remaining roughly the same.[6]

Meanwhile, 55 per cent and 44 per cent of the voters polled by MORI reported that they felt that they had too little information about their local candidate and policies of the parties respectively. Only 25 per cent felt that they had insufficient information about the party leaders.[7]

Voters just don't seem to be getting the information they demand through the mass media.

4 *Third parties* • A key indicator of voter alienation from conventional politics is the number of voters opting for third parties – essentially a protest vote. The set of choices on offer of parties who have a chance of forming a government is too narrow and hence insufficiently close to the electorate's political choice-set. So they feel able to use a vote as protest.

The UK Independence Party saw its vote increase by 1.2 per cent, the BNP by 0.1 per cent, and the Green Party by 0.4 per cent. These are tiny figures but they are a small indicator of potential discontent with conventional politics.

5 *Local issues* • The Wyre Forest election deserves a special mention because it is the exception that proves the rule. Turnout in Wyre Forest reached 68 per cent in a local campaign dominated by a single issue – the fate of the local hospital (although turnout was actually down by 7 per cent on 1997). The single independent MP elected in 1997 had won essentially on an issue of personal ethics.

As the Wyre Forest campaign was dominated by a political issue which the local electorate felt they had no influence over, it marks an interesting feature of alienation. It is important not to push this example too far – Wyre Forest was a unique case – but it is a feature of the last election that needs to be highlighted.

6 *Activist absence* • A general sense of alienation and impotence when faced with politics as currently configured can be seen most starkly in the increased difficulty that parties are having in motivating their members and supporters to become actively involved in election campaigns.

A recent MORI survey[8] shows that only 14 per cent of the electorate had been canvassed by a representative of a local party (down from 24 per cent in 1997 and 30 per cent in 1992). Three per cent had helped a local party in 2001 (down from 4 per cent in 1997 and 6 per cent in 1992).

These figures match the anecdotal evidence of those who were involved in the campaign this time – it was significantly more difficult to motivate local supporters than was the case in 1997 (itself worse than 1992). It is not just the electorate that feel less motivated by traditional political institutions and processes but it is the activists as well.

When putting all this evidence together, it is difficult to argue anything other than that the electorate is increasingly disengaging from the political process. Of course, this disengagement could be contentment or fatalism but as we shall see in the following section these explanations are complacent at best, misleading at worst.

All of this is occurring despite no overall decline in the interest that people have in politics. They express their politics in different ways – consumer choice, direct action, and passivity towards conventional politics – but they are alienated. Our task is to now explain why.

1.2.2 • Explaining a disengaging electorate

The multitude of explanations, theories and suppositions aiming at explaining voter disengagement can be placed in four categories: the circumstantial, the institutional, theories claiming the 'end of politics', and those looking to the media-political complex to explain alienation. One thing binds all these theories aside from the circumstantial: voters are alienated from the conventional political process. The circumstantial hypothesis will be analysed first followed by a review of the other theories.

1.2.2.1 • *Why would you vote in an election that was pre-determined?* On election night, Ministers were falling over themselves to brush aside low turnout by claiming that the 'evidence on the doorstep' is that people knew who was going to win and this was a severe de-motivating factor. You only have to look in safe Labour seats where the fall in turnout was the largest to find evidence for this.

The purpose of this analysis is to explain *change*. Why do more people, and especially more young people, seem to be alienated from the political process than was previously the case? The problem with this hypothesis centring on the circumstances of this election is that it just doesn't seem to explain change adequately.

Undoubtedly, close elections are more likely to induce excitement in the election and focus the minds of the electorate in picking an alternative. There was a turnout of 78 per cent in the close election of February 1974 compared with 72 per cent in 1970 (a low turnout that interestingly contributed to a surprise result). Turnout in the Conservative landslide victory of 1983 was 3.3 per cent lower than 1979. The turnout in the close election of 1992 was 2.4 per cent higher than in 1987. However, turnout in the close election of 1964 was actually 1.6 per cent down on the more predictable election of 1959.[9] So the law is not cast in stone.

If one looks at electoral turnout from the end of the war until 1992, the figures seem to be pretty trendless, i.e. they shift in accordance with peculiar circumstances. Turnout moves up and down and doesn't seem to vary by more than about six points between elections.

However, after the 1992 election something strange seems to occur. Firstly, turnout declines by 6.3 per cent between 1992 and 1997 (at the upper end but within post-war variations) and then falls by a *further 12 per cent* between 1997 and 2001. This fall is *unprecedented* in the post-war era. The sheer scale of decline should alert us to the fact that there may be something more than circumstances behind the fall.

Of course, it may just be that voter turnout has suddenly become more volatile (due to factors such as declining identification with political parties as we become more middle-class). We will not know for sure whether this is the case or not until we have another close election (in which case we could expect the voting rate to soar). However, evidence from across the Atlantic Ocean does not bode well for this supposition – turnout in the extremely close Presidential election of 2001 was just 2.4 per cent higher than turnout in Bill Clinton's landslide victory of 1996. This figure has neat parallels with the 2 per cent increase in turnout between the 1987 and 1992 elections in the UK. It would be complacent to wait for absolutely incontrovertible statistical evidence before acting on what could be a genuine challenge to the legitimacy of our democracy.

Furthermore, there is little evidence that those who stayed away from the polls were 'contented' with the government. They may have thought a Labour victory inevitable, but surely if this was to your displeasure, a rational strategy would be to vote to minimise the majority of the party making it's programme more difficult to implement. Opinion poll evidence shows that the government has only had a positive approval rating once in the last year (and that was after the General Election). They are fortunate that William Hague's approval ratings were even worse.[10]

This evidence shows that the 'inevitability' argument is probably stronger than the 'contented' argument. However, it would be a divergence from historical trend and available evidence to suppose that circumstances explain the rapid decline in turnout over the last nine years.

1.2.2.2 • *Change the procedures and they will come* • While it is easy to see why circumstantial arguments for explaining low turnout suit the politicians of the winning party, it is equally interesting to see how those interested in constitutional reform have seized the debate about low turnout for their own ends.

Institutional explanations come in a variety of forms – from procedural to constitutional – with the arguments bound by a single supposition. The electorate are not voting because the actual means of voting (i.e. the way that the electorate connects to the political process) is either inconvenient or ineffective in its results. People want to vote but the voting system and procedures are out of date.

There are a number of proposals that have been put forward to reverse this situation:

- *Procedural*: compulsory voting, different forms of voting (on-line voting, telephone voting, mobile voting booths etc.), easier registration
- *Constitutional*: proportional representation, devolution
- *Educational*: teaching citizenship in schools
- *Legal*: electoral and fundraising law (e.g. reform of party election broadcasts).

The problem with these explanations is that they do not, by any stretch of the imagination, explain why people are *increasingly* disengaged from politics. They may be worthy in and of their own right but they do not adequately explain the phenomena that we are actually experiencing.

Our society demands more convenience. If trust can be constructed for new and innovative forms of voting then all the better, but it will have little impact on the voting figures – it will change the *way* not *whether* people vote. Half a million more people voted by post in 2001 due to laws making the process of applying for postal votes easier still but there is little evidence that these people would not have voted anyway.

Devolution may help citizens to re-engage with local institutions but the problem of how local government can create a space for itself in the new media era will remain. Proportional representation may allow people to express a protest vote more obviously, but coalition governments can be as difficult to dislodge as those in first-past-the-post systems (and often more so). Countries that have proportional representation are experiencing exactly the same problems as Britain and the United States.

Compulsory voting would simply be a form of collective political denial. Individuals would be fined for the failure of the political system to connect with them and we would be left with a voting system that was superficially healthy but a democracy that was decaying from within.

Teaching citizenship in schools is desirable, if only to imbue citizens of the future with a sense that politics and political participation do matter. However, it doesn't change the environment in which politics operates, i.e. an environment where new media images and commitments dominate.

One area where institutional reforms may help is in the relationship between politics and the new media. It is clear that the party election broadcast is an anachronism. Strict advertising restrictions for political organisation is a luxury that the era of mass media could afford. The era of multiple communications channels with diversified audiences demands a less restrictive regime where political organisations are permitted to target audiences where they are, with messages that are personalised and engaging rather than generalised messages to uninterested audiences. This will, of course, raise issues of party funding that will need to be addressed maturely rather than in the puritanical fashion which precedes much of the debate about the funding of politics. We may have capped party funding at precisely the wrong time.

The risk is that the realm of political communications could be about to become even more restrictive. A storm cloud on the horizon was innocuously inserted into the Electoral Commissions report into the General Election: 'It will be important to ensure that the use of the internet in campaigning is regulated in the same way as traditional campaigning.' Surely, libel and incitement laws are sufficient?

What the institutional arguments amount to is a set of proposals which are desirable to varying degrees but which will, ultimately, have little effect on voter engagement with politics.

1.2.2.3 • *Politics after 'the end of politics'* • Narratives about the end of politics at the hands of big business are currently very much in vogue. It is not difficult to see why. Dramatic images of mass demonstrations, riots, protests, and occasional anarchy occupy a space in the media in comparison with which politicians seem irrelevant. These are complex times but it is reassuring to have an anti-capitalist, anti-globalisation and anti-big business/brand totem around which to mobilise.

The books enter the best-seller lists, the writers become international celebrities and, dare I say it, brands in their own right. In the past year, three books have woven and spread the narrative in particular – *Captive state: the corporate takeover of Britain* by George Monbiot, *No Logo* by Naomi Klein, and *The Silent Takeover: global capitalism and the death of democracy* by Noreena

Hertz. Though amorphous, they have the same message at their core (albeit from different angles): politics and the people are no longer in control, big business calls all the shots.

For purposes of demonstration, I will analyse Noreena Hertz's contribution here. *The Silent Takeover* is an ideal choice as it explicitly links an increase in corporate power both in the public, global and private realms with increases in political disengagement and voter alienation.

According to Dr Hertz:

People have lost faith in politics, because they no longer know what governments are good for. Thanks to the steady withdrawal of the state over the past 20 years from the public sphere, it is corporations, not governments, that increasingly define the public realm.[11]

Politicians and political discourse have moved into an insipid consensus in which corporate power has been acquiesced with rather than tempered. Corporates use political donations for self-interested ends (and politicians allow them to do so), the entire agenda of 'big business' is promulgated by the owners of mass media who seek to perpetuate the politics of the corporate over the people. It is the end of politics.[12]

Consequently, the electorate was offered this compromise and it is little wonder they respond with withering silence or direct action. The consensus centres around:

A reduced state, with an ever greater dependence on corporations for solutions.[13]

While there is scant evidence that there is a generalised sense that politics is no longer powerful and, consequently, voting is irrelevant, there is significant evidence of localised concern at the use of the private sector in the delivery of public services (evidence shows that the vast majority of the electorate believe voting to be purposeful in general). However, it is premature to link these localised concerns into a broad narrative of a 'corporate' or 'silent takeover' of British political life.

The linkages between corporate and political power and then voter alienation are rather deterministically assumed in these accounts of the current political environment. By way of comparison, the putative 'consensus' of the 1950s had no measurable impact on political engagement at all.

These narratives also assume (again in a rather axiomatic fashion reminiscent of previous materialist critiques of political economy) that anything that favours business is immediately to the detriment of the people. Undoubtedly, there are circumstances in all political systems where a lack of knowledge, misjudgement or, occasionally corruption (though rather more occasional than is assumed) leads to inappropriate policy. As we will see in *The Contagious Campaign • (part 2)*, this can lead to the government of the day getting a bloody nose, but to characterise this as a 'corporate takeover' is to over-egg the pudding somewhat.

Governments actually enjoy a significant amount of power to finance and manage public services in the way they wish given certain parameters of international political economy. One just has to compare the way the welfare state is financed and managed in the Scandinavian countries with the British approach to see that. Sweden could hardly be described as in crisis.[14] Political choice is actual and understood and there are significant differences between the approaches of the two main parties in Britain to public policy.

Given these genuine differences within political competition, we must look elsewhere if we are to fully explain the agency at play which may blur the distinctions of political choice. We must look to the prism that is the media-political complex.

1.2.2.4 • *The media-political complex* • 'If 1997 is a wake-up call, 2001 is a sign that we've all overslept', [Richard Tait, ITN editor-in-chief.][15]

Mud has been slung from both sides – politicians and media – in a blame game for increasing voter alienation. The politicians, for their part, accuse the media of trivialising politics, focusing on gaffes, trying to catch politicians out with aggressive interviewing that is off-putting to the general public, obsessing with personalities and personal disagreement, reporting the 'froth' rather than substance of politics.

In retaliation, the media (both print and broadcast), criticise politicians for dispensing unpredictable favours in an effort to manipulate the media by defining access, attempting to control the media through prescriptive and dull political messages which infringe genuine political discussion and using 'off-the-record' (i.e. unattributable) briefings to create personal agendas.

Six of one, half a dozen of the other, one could say. One thing is clear, despite mutual antipathy, the relationship between the modern media and politics can be defined as one of creative destruction. The relationship between politicians and journalists, though occasionally descending into mutual loathing, is one of mutual need and attempted mutual manipulation. More than any other, the relationship between politician and journalist/broadcaster can be said to epitomise the era of mass media.

What is equally clear is that while this relationship is alive and thriving, it is increasingly one that is separated from the real experiences and expectations of the electorate. Some news reporting and analysis is sublime and many politicians are candid and articulate, but this is not the norm. Increasingly, the arcane relationship and set of dependencies exist in an environment with its own set of symbols, language, referents and meanings. Unfortunately, this is a culture, defined in the era of mass media, separate from the cultural symbols, values and expectations of the electorate itself.

Of all the theories is this the most apt and valid? There is little doubt that the electorate perceives politics and politicians to exist in a near parallel universe (where flickers of recognition occur but reality seems strangely corrupted). A focus group during the 2001 election produced comments such as, 'I think they [the politicians] are not involved with the public – they just talk to the media', 'I felt it was the media who helped make it a one way ticket. No new issues were expressed – there wasn't enough difference between the parties', and 'No-one is looking at what they are saying ... decent, honest people are derided and condemned by so-called clever journalists. The media journalists think they are kings'.[16]

It is far too easy to assume that because we are no longer experiencing the grand historical clash of ideology that was socialism versus capitalism, political conflict has etiolated. Far from it, any objective analysis of party platforms at the last election shows that there are actually quite significant differences in major areas of policy – public services, taxation, international engagement, pensions, education policy and so the list goes on. However, as is clear from the above quotations, there is a *perception* that there are few differences. An intermediary between politics and the people is diminishing genuine party competition.

However, while these theories add description to the issue of voter alienation, this is a situation that has been around for a long time, but these theories are still inadequate in explaining why people are suddenly tired of it. The cosy relationship between journalists and media and the 'media management' operations of political parties have existed for decades. 'Media management' may have been epitomised by new Labour but why the sudden change in voter engagement with the political process?

The answer is, of course, that while the media political complex could survive in the era of mass media (albeit with increasing strains), in the era of new media, it is seen as a cultural residue from another time by an ever more demanding, conditional and critical audience. Politics and the traditional news media largely exist in a time and space that the electorate has moved beyond.

1.3 • The onset of the new media era

The Age of Access . . . is bringing with it a new type of human being. The young people of the new 'protean' generation are far more comfortable conducting business and engaging in social activity in the worlds of electronic commerce and cyberspace, and they adapt easily to the many simulated worlds that make up the cultural economy. Theirs is world that is more theatrical than ideological and oriented more to a play ethos than to a work ethos.

[*The Age of Access*, Jeremy Rifkin][17]

➡ While increasing voter alienation has multiple causes, politics can't afford to ignore the possibility that its whole structure and underlying assumptions may not be particularly well-adapted to the modern cultural environment. The central argument is that the interaction of culture, technology and global communications has shifted the rules and parameters of collective space in a way that is little understood by today's political class.

If we are to find ways to reconnect, then it is imperative that we seek to understand the cultural shift that all organisations are facing – political, voluntary, corporate or cultural. A reconnection can only be achieved if it is understood what we should be reconnected to. The nerds have not triumphed, it's just that the space they first occupied has been invaded and colonised. This modern empire is the increasingly entwined global entertainment and communications giants. They are the gate-keepers to the collective and cultural space of the new media.

This argument is not one of technology, it is one concerning the cultural predilections, preferences, instincts and symbols of the younger generations in particular. We did not enter the era of new media when the internet started. In fact, its germination was well before the early 1990s. MTV and cable television were the first manifestations of the new media. It is just that it has spread to other technologies and other environments – to the internet, digital television and satellite, palm tops and 3G mobile networks, the computer gaming industries, and mass entertainment. The cultural disposition of those growing up in the new media age has burst out of technology. Fantasies, dramatic fragments, self-assembled mosaics of experience and entertainment, social networks sustained by the shared symbols of what Baudrillard would call 'hyper-reality' all perpetuate themselves in a world where what may seem 'virtual' is actually the highest form of reality.

Cultures of the new media age are propagated by the reproduction of fragile and contextualised networks. While global communications giants are the gate-keepers of a pastiche of flickering images; subjects themselves are the guardians of their fluid and interactive engagements with new media. If you are knocking on the outside of the subject-defined reality you had better know the entry code or outside you will remain.

This is a world where politics matters but also doesn't. It has effect but is not noticed. Issues matter but political institutions seem not to. The public realm shrinks like the spiritual realm did before it. It is a world in which politics is in danger of losing its perceived meaning. It is a world of political disconnection.

1.3.1 • Mass media versus new media

It is hardly worth commenting that modern politics is dominated by mass media. When voters get a good deal of the political output from papers and television and, concurrently, political parties find it increasingly difficult to motivate activists and they are restricted from advertising freely in the media, it is entirely obvious that a close relationship will develop between politicians and journalists.

However, as media expands and diversifies, it seems that political discourse is reserved for a tiny aspect of the media. While that media defines an ever larger portion of our *collective* space it occupies a rapidly diminishing area of our *cultural space*. In other words, politics has lost its captive audience.

The table below compares features of a collective and cultural environment defined by the mass media and one defined by the new media. It will be immediately obvious that we are moving away from the former towards the latter:

Mass media	New media
• Small number of channels	• Infinite number of channels
• Linearity	• Interactivity
• One programme at a time	• Multiple programmes/multi-tasking
• A handful of access points (radio, television, newspapers)	• Multiple and varied access points
• High degree of regulation	• Largely unregulated and difficult to regulate
• Planned and programmed	• Spontaneous
• Viewers	• Participants
• Occasional	• All-encompassing
• Entertainment	• Experience

It is nearly impossible to say when the media shifted its form from characterising mass to new media but what is certain is that the shift has been occurring for some time. What is equally certain is that the shift is gathering pace and the majority of young people inhabit a cultural space that is far more reminiscent of the new media than the mass media ideal type.

Just in case any confusion remains, this cultural space is not defined by any specific technology or set of technologies. The characteristic of new media is that it happens everywhere and always. Individuals define themselves in the context of networks and these networks are cohered by shared symbols and meaning that are often ungrounded in real events, facts and places. A great deal of modern culture occurs between people over the phone, in the street, on e-mail as well as through digital television, Play Station 2, and the internet.

Compare a typical phone conversation now to 20 years ago. Phone conversations tended to be between family and good friends and would be relatively infrequent and personal. The modern phone conversation takes place over a mobile phone – the modern badge of citizenship. It will start with an enquiry about the whereabouts of the individual (in the dramatic construction that is often the young person's cultural life, scene-setting is important). An exchange about someone's love life, family life, or fashion definition will ensue. It will not be clear whether the conversation revolves around the participants in the conversation or someone else or a celebrity or a TV programme recounted. It will last a few minutes and then be followed with half-a-dozen text messages or so. What has occurred is not a conversation between friends but an entertainment connection – the participants are creating drama and meaning for each other. They are directors and occasional actors.

A television commercial by the mobile phone company, One-to-One, epitomised the new world quite brilliantly. 'Who would you have a One-to-One with?' was its theme. The subject in the advert generally got to speak to someone who'd inspired them. That is what it is about. The new media era is about instant and constructed satiation. It is a formidable task for politics to seek a space and legitimacy in this environment.

1.3.2 • The new media generation

Jeremy Rifkin, in his seminal work *The Age of Access*, argues that fundamental shifts in the means of human communication are always accompanied by shifts in human consciousness. What has occurred is that humans whose primary cognitive and emotional development was in the modern environment display a specific disposition.

Faced with multiple networks of interests and shared culture they treat their life as a process rather than event, continual inventing and re-inventing themselves to fit shifting and multiple environments. All life is for the present – all history, culture and personality is drawn into the now and not the could be. In Rifkin's own words:

The fast pace of a hyper-real, nanosecond culture shortens the individual and collective temporal horizon to the immediate moment. Traditions and legacies become fading interests. What counts is 'now', and what's important is being able to feel and experience the moment.[18]

What is true of the cultural realm is rapidly becoming equally true of the political realm. To be clear, political discourse and process has become subsumed into mass media over the past decades. It is about to become one reality amongst millions in the new media era.

In political terms, each of the generations now of voting age approach the political realm with different expectations and utilities as the table below demonstrates. I have included the column 'consumer values' because political action is increasingly undertaken in the world of consumption as well as democratic politics.

Generation	Characteristics	Political motivation	Consumer values
Elvis and the Beatles	50 and above, family values, community, locality, tradition	Duty and traditional political identification	Consumption as necessity
Madonna	25–50, Materialistic, accumulative, self-interested, 'Thatcher's children'	Instrument of self-interest	Consumption as ostentation
Gorillaz	18–25, experience-seeking, entertainment primary motivation, highly social	Personal expression	Personal expression

From the above typology (and, it should be emphasised, that it is a typology and not a general description of all people and motivations within the categories!), it can be deduced that a different type of politics is likely to better engage with each group and its 'consciousness.'

Politics conducted through the traditional media outlets, on terrestrial television channels and through the press will only measure as a blip on the radar screen of this group. Billboard advertising, though seen by 61 per cent of the electorate during the election (Electoral Commission, 2001, 66) will only be seen as a flickering light with generalised messages of good hope and foreboding. Politics, like culture, will have to prove its meaning to this group. Messages such as 'we'll save the health service' or 'we'll manage the economy well' will become less effective. The language employed in politics will have to be more targeted, personalised, about their life experiences. Policy proposals will have to be linked to definite outcomes and these outcomes will have to be proven to be life enhancing. Pre-determined messages will still find their way into daily news bulletins but their dry and general nature will make it increasingly difficult for the messages to escape into the wider cultural environment.

The real political stars of the future will be those who deploy the political architecture with the aim of having a series of near intimate one-to-one conversations with voters. For those who fail to achieve this, well, the mobile phone is ringing and MTV is waiting.

1.3.3 • Just a matter of communication?

This analysis and the prescriptions that come out of it assume a level of political competence in the actual transformation of policy into positive outcome. If the innovations and institutional management of politicians is ineffective or inappropriate then no amount of consummate communication can convince. As Tom Bentley argued in a recent paper:

The challenge of a new politics is not just to provide a language which can capture people's values and aspirations and clarify the issues of the day. The real challenge is to connect those emerging values and priorities with systems of organisation which can make a difference to people's daily lives.[19]

If we lived in a world that was purely characterised by a kind of post-modern dystopia where reality did not exist and fantasy prevailed, then actual policy delivery may not be so important. While a good portion of the electorate is showing post-modern characteristics in much of their cultural lives, there still is a need for a politics that delivers. One thing that the internet does allow for is for the rapid proliferation of information. Much of the information is tendentious but if you are not delivering then a created reality may be one of incompetence and failure. As any politician knows, perceived competence is the difference between political success and failure and perception is grounded in delivery more often than not.

We should be grateful that communication only works in a general environment of substance and competence. If the alternative was the case, i.e. politics as a series of theatrically constructed realities, then it is unlikely that it would matter much. Moreover, our political systems are facing ever more complex problems of social preference over ideology. Issues of personal privacy, environmental caution, defining a role and delivery capability for public services, re-distribution of cultural capital and educational resources between sections of the community and access to the cultural artefacts of the modern age are all political issues that are pressing and require real public debate before politics can act with legitimacy and authority.

Political space may be on the verge of being sucked into a new media environment – an environment it has to seek an understanding of, if it is to replenish itself – but it still has to find new and creative means of creating a better society.

1.4 • Communication in the era of new media

➡ Skills, leadership and knowledge are no longer sufficient to succeed in the modern world. You have to be a performer, empathiser, creator, coalition builder, and teacher as well. The demands on governments and businesses are increasing in complexity. Governments are no longer just expected to manage the economy and public services more efficiently. They also have to contend with the shifting global issues of the day – privacy, access, cultural poverty, networked crime, ethical enterprise, environmental degradation – in a context where authority is often negotiated rather than legislated for.

In this world of complexity and search for subjective expression and meaning, there is an ever-greater tendency towards the personal and particular. Just ask Marks and Spencer about that. And yet the communication practices of our major political parties and many of the largest companies have barely shifted in form and fundamental assumptions. There is little doubt that they are increasingly professionalised, but they are just not personal. If you are not speaking to me then why are you speaking at all?

Some core principles that might inform the communication of the future follow. We are still waiting for a communication to catch up with a future that has already arrived.

1.4.1 • Home is where the heart is

It is probably one of the greatest challenges of modern communication to find an expression and series of symbols adapted to the collective space of the new media era. It is no longer simply a matter of phrasing policies, targeting messages and getting into the right papers for swing voters.

If politics is allowed to become an irrelevance then we will start to live in an extremely volatile age where political programmes will be increasingly difficult to implement over time and public institutions will suffer a crisis of credibility. Imagine being a Prime Minister in an environment where nothing you do is recognised or understood and elections become a nail-biting moment where you hope that your opponent doesn't manage to capture the imagination of a voting public diminishing in number. Politics will become a casino rather than a democratic process.

Politics has to enter the playground of people's lives and recognise where they are, the language they use, and what their commitments are. You will get a single moment to make your case; you had better be ready for that moment and know who you are speaking to and why they are there.

This doesn't just go for politics, it also goes for public services. Companies have created sophisticated customer relationship management (CRM) systems. The public sector has completely and utterly failed to import these models which both deliver and respond to individual preferences. Companies have done it because it helps give them the edge over competitors and creates loyal customers. It could be argued that many public services have no competition. Think again. Not only is the route of private sector alternatives still available but if public services are not seen to deliver then their political legitimacy is undermined. Forget Public Private Partnerships, a failure to adapt to the new era could mean privatisation of whole swathes of the public sector hitherto considered as sacrosanct.

The problem of re-engaging the young is of real concern. The only buzz in politics is outside party politics. The complacent assumption is that this is just the young being young. They will re-engage when they get older and are paying taxes and have responsibilities. Maybe, but the more likely explanation, given the cultural shift that is occurring from mass to new media, is that modern partisan politics is just not relevant anymore. Whenever the young actually look at the political debate they see and hear a group of people using language that is alien to them. Key symbolic issues seem to reinforce the view that politics is a world apart: tuition fees (the manner of the introduction of tuition fees has severely harmed the image of this government amongst large sections of youth), a failure to have a realistic debate about drug and drinking laws, and the increasing pressure of education by measurement.

Very few cool people are involved in politics and if you are involved in politics it is almost the definition of being not cool. A free concert held by Channel 4 cricket on Brighton beach featuring FatBoy Slim shows that even cricket can re-connect better with young people than politics!

It is no longer simply enough to have a few party political broadcasts, the odd free leaflet, and hope your media relations do the rest. The evidence shows that these methods combined can hit a significant proportion of the electorate. However, it hits them with broad political messages which have little meaning to their daily lives more often than not.

Politics has to go beyond these 'channels' and enter the world of digital television, mobile phones, the internet, music festivals and text messaging. It has to not only sell a set of policies that relate to people's lives but also become part of their self-expression. It is now important, rather than presenting long lists of policies from which voters can choose what suits them, to provide personalised and targeted messages. Generalised sound-bites are becoming an increasingly blunt tool. Targeted and personal messages are increasingly becoming the expectation of the new media generation. The technology is there, use it.

1.4.2 • Know why your audience is there

For a few years at the end of the 1990s, one of the most embarrassing spectacles in politics would occur on an annual basis. Until John Prescott was drenched in ice by Chumbawumba, there would be an annual procession of the great and good from both political parties to the Brit Awards. Almost as embarrassing, is the appearance of politicians on Saturday morning TV from time to time (maybe the strategy is to target the kid's parents but it is painful to watch).

It should be stated categorically that the argument is not that politicians should try to look cool. Their job is to look after their constituents, communicate political programmes, govern, that sort of thing. If you have to try to look cool then you are not.

However, political messages and symbols should try to infiltrate the multiple channels and interaction of new media. In order to achieve this, politics needs to find carriers. Celebrity or image montages that use the non-verbal code that is much of today's entertainment to spark a little interest in what 'Labour' or 'Conservative' means (the Conservative Party's brand is especially crusty for a number of reasons and this is reflected in the average age of party membership).

We can be reactionary and say that politics should maintain the dignity of the status quo. There is no dignity in irrelevance.

Celebrity and imagery are the grammar of the new media era. The hyper-link, viewer poll, or phone-in forms its punctuation. Politicians are spoilt from an early age into believing that they have a right to be heard and are great men of history in the making. In the conditionality of new media, this is simply no longer the case. We require a form of political communication far more sophisticated than anything we have seen.

Behaviour is as important as presence. Just because someone is partaking in a channel of new media, it doesn't mean that they want to be engaged in political interaction. If they are there for music and light entertainment make the judgement if it is relevant for you to be there at all. If they are there for news and information, your opportunity may be better. These are the complex judgements of our time: where is your audience, why are they there, and what is the form of communication that will appeal to them? Sport, global activism, news and commerce have made the move into this new environment, why can't politics?

1.4.3 • Be prepared to get active

The point has already been made that generalised political communication no longer interests audiences even if they are exposed to them. If campaigns – corporate and political – are to succeed in a new media environment then it is essential that they use all the resources available to them in searching out audiences in spaces where they may be interested. This mission is one of tactics and organisation.

Any campaign that will effectively target an audience floating around in new media space must have the following elements:

1 A new media unit right at the head of any campaigning group. The group would be party to central strategic planning and decision-making. It would have the power to interpret central political messages and creatively target them at key audiences using multiple technologies – on and off-line. The 'Head of New Media' would be a post as prestigious as Head of press, public affairs or PR. All new media output would be created specifically with a particular medium in mind.

Central government communications would have a similar post with a similar remit. The function of the post would be to develop an awareness of the new media environment throughout the public sector and integrate that thinking with corporate and communications planning.

The first principle of the post would be, 'the shift to new media is a cultural rather than technological one embodying a more diverse and challenging environment for government communications. A relevant, targeted and personalised strategy going to heart of corporate planning must, therefore, be devised.'

2 The new media environment is ultimately networked. Networks are conditional and so individuals must feel emotionally engaged if they are to participate. However, we can't wait for perfection in communications before a political network is constructed. Campaigning organisations

must start to forge a space for themselves in the new cultural environment.

Every single sinew of your organisation, from activists to employees, shop stewards to check-out staff, must be geared towards building that network. You need e-mail addresses and you need as much information about people who are interested in your cause as possible. Any regional office that doesn't collect 1,000 e-mail addresses a year should be fined. Demographic and contact information, conditionally given, is the currency of the new media era.

Any political party that goes into the next general election with less than 1 million e-mail addresses has failed both to orient its organisation to the new cultural environment and to engage with the electorate.

3   A strong creative vibe backed up by significant and reliable research. The environment is more complex and complex times call for complex measures. Specific research into the attitudes of sections of the community to political and communications products must be undertaken regularly and thoroughly. This is not the triumph of focus group but the survival of politics.

Regular research should be disseminated to creative people who are skilled at manipulating images, language, celebrity and humour to spark interest and awareness. Any communications department will just have to trust people with a proven creative record. Nothing would be worse than a highly effective montage followed by a head and shoulders shot of a politician saying 'vote for me and I'll make the world a better place.'

4 The space of politics has to widen. Quite simply, if politics fails to break out of the cocoon of Westminster, and onto web-sites, mobile phones, and the entire space of new media then it will become an increasingly arcane activity.

5 Eventually, the new media unit will be the campaign itself just as new media will be society itself. Until then (and that day may be decades away), it is important that everything the new unit does is integrated with press, PR and lobbying strategies. It must have the ability to produce its own material for particular media but the overall message and information must be consistent across the entire campaign.

Planning will become more important. It will no longer be a case of, 'we are focusing on 'x issue' can you stick it on a web-site?' Target groups, their cultural disposition, their interests and your brand image in their eyes must be considered.

1.4.4 • New times, new institutions

The current institutional configuration of the British political process is harming the ability of political parties to connect in the new media era. It creates an atmosphere where politics has to duck and dive into the public consciousness meaning that politics is no longer a dialogue between those who elect and those who are elected. From what has preceded, it should be clear that these institutional changes will not be sufficient but they will be necessary.

Quite simply, politics has to find a space for itself that is free from the closing gates of the current political world.

The necessary changes include:

1 Party Political Broadcasts and Party Election Broadcasts should be ended. Instead, an 'airtime' bank should be set up for the parties to use on any channel broadcasting in the UK.
2 Any regulation of politics on the internet should be fiercely resisted. Data protection, libel and incitement laws are sufficient.
3 Mobile phone operators granted operation licenses in the UK should be required to give the parties one text message each during a general election campaign.
4 Any cable franchise should be required to give access to their interactive channels to political parties.
5 The cost of these changes may mean that we have a public debate about limits to political spending of political parties. The argument is that political parties are legitimate agents of democratic competition and, as they are locked out of so much of the modern cultural terrain, democracy may not be functioning as well as it should.

Some of these policies may seem illiberal. However, we've had compulsory political broadcasts for decades now with very little comment. This set of institutions is necessary for the political sphere to redefine and recreate itself. It is the nature of public space that it is often in conflict with private property. This is as true in new media era as it was in the industrial economy. And a few text messages every four or five years is hardly a huge price to pay for democracy.

If after all these institutional changes, politics is still having difficulty connecting, then it only has itself to blame.

1.5 • Democracy without citizenship

➥ Increasingly, politicians have realised that culture is no longer separate from politics. Political action is no longer simply a matter of plucking your socio-economic ideology off the shelf and ruthlessly applying it. Unemployment, poverty, organisational failure, educational achievement, social support are all dependent to a greater or lesser degree on the 'culture' variable. In other words, the language, values, expectations and symbols of communities are understood to be determinants of the success or failure of political action.

Just as politics has to engage with the institutions of civic society and the people themselves in order to craft legitimate and impactful solutions to ingrained problems, it has to seek to communicate with clusters of particular culture. The politics of ideas, policies, and communication all sit alongside each other as they always have done. These are the resources of power.

The 1970s saw a threat to all these three resources. The current environment, an environment defined by complexity and change, places severe strains on politics of ideas and policies. However, the signs are that, albeit with the difficulty one would expect from a complexity environment, politics is finding ways to generate ideas and discover purposeful policies. Political competition, far from being moribund and entering a new era of consensus, is actually quite healthy in the competition between the two major political forces. New Labour has meaning and so does the modern Conservative Party. You wouldn't believe that from watching the news coverage in the general election where all politicians are thrown into the liquidiser of mass media. It is little wonder that when all discussion is of personalities and personal conflict, all politicians seem the same.

There is choice. However, people are increasingly turned off by the way in which these choices are communicated. The politics of communications is failing and this could have potentially catastrophic consequences for the state of democracy in Britain and most other western democracies who are facing exactly the same problems.

Quite simply, politics no longer fits in the cultural environment in which it finds itself and the fit will get worse. It seems that today's young will not accept the political hand-me-downs of their parents. They won't accept them because their tastes and expectations are different. Politics needs a new style, new outlets, brighter, bolder, more personal and more direct. Without this understanding of the new culture, the culture of new media, the generation who breathe new media, will simply find its clothes elsewhere. Politics in the new media era will simply be an echo and momentary flicker from a time gone by.

Liberal democracies rely on the concept of citizenship in order to function with authority and legitimacy. A failure to understand and re-engage with the changed cultural environment can mean only one thing. Politics may have to function in a democracy without citizenship.

1.6 • Acknowledgements

➥ Special thanks must go to Stephen Edwards whose invaluable research provided the back-bone to this chapter – he showed creativity beyond the call of duty at every stage. Teresa Clegg deserves a special mention for having the patience and good humour to support me in putting these ideas together. Mark Hoda and Muriel Desaulles both contributed greatly to the final copy of both this chapter and the other chapters in the book- thank you.

Notes

[1] Castells, Manuel, *The Rise of the Network Society*, (England, Blackwell, 1996).
[2] Bentley, Tom, *It's Democracy, Stupid: An Agenda for Self-government*, http://www.demos.co.uk/demostupid.htm, 2001.
[3] Hertz, Noreena, *The Silent Takeover: global capitalism and the death of democracy*, (England, Heinemann, 2001) and Monbiot, George, *Captive State: the corporate takeover of Britain*, (England, Macmillan, 2001).

[4] Electoral Commission, *Election 2001*, http://www.electoral-commission.gov.uk/publications.htm, July 2001.

[5] ibid

[6] Golding, Peter and Deacon, David, *An election that many watched but few enjoyed*, http://www.guardian.co.uk/Archive/Article/0,4273,4202346,00.html, 12 June 2001.

[7] Electoral Commission op.cit.

[8] MORI/ Mortimore, Roger, *Politics on the Canvas(s)*, http://www.mori.com/digest/2001/c010803.shtml, 3 August 2001.

[9] Butler, David, *Putting turnout in perspective*, http://www.hansard-society.org.uk/voterapathy.htm, March 2001.

[10] MORI, *Satisfaction ratings*, http://www.mori.com/polls/trends/satisf12.shtml, July 2001.

[11] Hertz, Noreena, *Why we must stay silent no longer*, http://www.guardian.co.uk/Archive/Article/0,4273,4167263,00.html, 8 April 2001.

[12] Hertz, Noreena, *The Silent Takeover: global capitalism and the death of democracy*, (England, Heinemann, 2001)

[13] Hertz, Noreena, *Why we must stay silent no longer*, http://www.guardian.co.uk/Archive/Article/0,4273,4167263,00.html, April 8th 2001.

[14] Turner, Adair, *Just Capital: the liberal economy* (England, Macmillan, 2001).

[15] Hodgson, Jessica, *TV newsmen warn of political 'crisis,'* http://www.guardian.co.uk/Archive/Article/0,4273,4203243,00.html, 13 June 2001.

[16] Electoral Commission op. cit.

[17] Rifkin, Jeremy, *The Age of Access: how the shift from ownership to access is transforming modern life*, (England, Penguin, 2001).

[18] ibid.

[19] Bentley op. cit.

2.

Measuring digital campaigns
Mike Bloxham and Andy Mayer

➡ The advent of interactive media has been accompanied by an alarming amount of well-documented hype and hysteria. From an investment community blinded by the dreams of young, headstrong entrepreneurs, to a media community obsessed by stories of online fraud and criminality, reactions to the potential offered by the internet, e-mail, WAP phones and interactive TV have been anything but measured.

Until now that is. Following the bursting of the internet bubble and the rude awakening that ensued for many, the overall view of new media is one of caution and healthy scepticism. Those who had previously rushed headlong in pursuit of riches – believing all was there for the taking – have succumbed to a strong dose of reality. Sanity has come to replace what was merely wishful thinking.

The result of this new-found sobriety has been the re-introduction of the 'old' rules of commerce and communication. Previously derided as the preserve of outdated monoliths awaiting their inevitable extinction, practices such as robust planning and evaluation have outlasted the mantra of 'the technology makes it possible, so people will do it' that underpinned so many so-called business plans. Companies that previously did not feel the need to either plan or evaluate properly have either gone to the wall or are now ardent advocates of both practices. The political arena has, of course, not been immune from this wave of unbridled enthusiasm. The UK General Election of 2001 was – according to many – set to be the country's first so-called e-election (some had even predicted the same for the election of 1997). It was not to be. At the same time, governments in most developed economies are striving to deliver as many public services online as possible – generally with little real understanding of whether or not citizens will actually change their behaviour and access them online. The public sector, just like the private sector, will find that interactive media works better for some purposes than others. Despite the sea change in the attitudes and practices that now permeate the new media community, one thing remains constant; the element that appeals most to users of new media and which influences behaviour more than any other is the sense of control and empowerment that most users feel. Rightly or wrongly, users perceive that with interactive media, they are better equipped to exercise choice, to interrogate and cross-check information, and to ignore or reject that which does not interest them. In almost all the research we have done, when asked what they like best about interactive media, respondents have cited a feeling of control as one of the principle benefits.

Empowerment is, however, a double-edged sword. Whilst to the individual it suggests a change in the balance of power between themselves and large organisations that seek to engage them – be they brands or political parties – to the organisations themselves, empowerment creates a different set of challenges. After all, the much-lauded two-way communications promised by the web can only bear fruit if both parties are interested in communicating.

The single most important factor influencing all communications online, therefore, is involvement. Without involvement there is no communication. Intelligently used, interactivity should enhance and extend the user's feeling of involvement and therefore their propensity to extend the dialogue, ultimately even to the extent of advocacy to others.

New media then, should be ideally suited to political campaigning. As one of the taboo subjects at polite dinner parties (outside of the political community), politics is renowned for stirring up strong feelings among even the avowedly apolitical; and strength of feeling is a pre-requisite for involvement.

Although campaign research can offer insights to inform the development of policy, this piece does not seek to address issues of policy research specifically. Instead we explore the use of a balanced scorecard approach to the development of a coherent and effective means of developing a campaign research architecture appropriate to individual campaigns.

2.1 • The political scorecard

➡ Bridging the knowledge gap between campaigners and voters

requires credible research. Credible research needs to be set in the context of a rigorous research architecture. The research architecture needs to be driven by the strategic objectives of the campaign, or rather the campaign by the strategic objectives of the organisation.

One of the most valuable methodologies available to communicate the importance of any campaign to key decision takers is the balanced scorecard (i.e. a set of criteria and goals against which a campaign can be evaluated). A balanced scorecard is a way in which the complexity of thousands of motivations, drivers and opinions can be reduced to the handful of key objectives that really make a difference.

In strategically focused business the scorecard is often divided into four sections:

- Financial
- Customer
- Internal
- Innovation and Learning.

This is particularly useful in digital business where purely financial indicators, such as cash-flow return on investment, are inadequate to determine the benefit of propositions (e.g. a website) that provide a combination of financial and communication benefits beyond the scope of the site itself.

For political campaigns this approach is helpful but not entirely applicable. Instead, we can look at the following criteria:

- Financial
- Opinion

- Supporters
- Evolution.

Within each section the political professional needs to understand the campaign drivers and from that strategic view develop the metrics that will (where possible) objectively measure the effectiveness of any initiatives.

2.1.1 • Why is the political scorecard valuable?

The political scorecard is a tool that can and should be applied to all areas of your campaigning – not just the digital. It is particularly relevant to digital campaigns however, at a time when so little is understood about why, how, or in what way these new communications channels are important. The scorecard, like any good message, conveys complexity in a language the target audience understands.

2.12 • What are the weaknesses of the political scorecard?

Effective score-carding requires long-term commitment and buy-in from senior decision-makers. It requires a commitment to regular research and a desire to communicate both successes and failures.

Many political organisations, particularly in the UK do not like to work in this fashion. Where organisations are driven by the vagaries of the daily press agenda; where funding is extremely irregular or where management is obsessively secretive; even aghast at the notion of assessment – the drive towards professional measurement can be a difficult although not insurmountable communications challenge.

In response to this challenge it is important to remember the purpose of a scorecard is not to dictate an external set of criteria that govern the right way to campaign. It is a partnership between stakeholders (both internal and external) to agree criteria by which to manage better political campaigns.

Or to put it another way, the campaign that can justify every action in the context of agreed objectives is more likely to thrive than simply survive.

2.2 • Financial perspective: digital campaigning and the bottom line

➡ Getting the money in is predominantly the remit of the professional fund-raiser. It is a skillset built around personal contact, persuasion and one in which digital professionals play a limited role.

Enabling a campaign website for e-commerce purposes is usually cosmetic compared to the benefit of a single cheque from a trust fund, however it is exceptionally useful for membership organisations where supporters can sign-up and amend their payments without the hassle of paper forms and cheques.

Example measures

Strategic Objective	Typical Measures	Example Digital metrics
Cost Management	Cost per supporter Headquarters cost	% member services online Digital infrastructure and support staff
Revenue	Membership contribution	£ per member
	Bequests	Unlikely to apply
	Corporate Membership	Unlikely to apply
	Fundraising	Returns from viral campaigns
	Sales of campaign materials	Returns from online store
Survival	Cash Flow	Unlikely to apply

2.3 • Opinion perspective: gaining mind-share

➡ The dominance of campaigning by the press officer mindset in the last decade has led to some pretty dubious measurement of success. The purpose of an effective press office is to get the right people saying the right things at the right time in the right publications. This leads some to quote column inches, rate cards or even volume of key opinion formers as their success criteria.

Strategically these can be important for internal morale, but should not be treated as credible measures of success.

There is no better measure of effectiveness than the simple answer to the question "Do you agree with x?'" or "Would you vote for y". The same is true online. Traffic isn't a measure of anything other than the effective proliferation of your presence. It says nothing about why your site is being visited, motivation or whether the visitor is convinced.

Example measures

Strategic Objective	Typical Measures	Example Digital metrics
Public Impact	Campaign Awareness Campaign Meaning	% of those online aware Those online understanding message
Effective Targeting	Core Support adoption Marginal Voter adoption	Viral forwarding statistics Sign-ups from target demographics
Personalisation	Meeting Needs Intensity	Personal Manifesto sign-ups Time online / advocacy

2.4 • Volunteer perspective: motivating the troops

➡ Healthy campaigns can expect to be robustly supported by volunteers, activists and advocates. The relative importance of these people to direct public communication will vary according to the campaign; clearly important for CND, less so for Nuclear Energy PR. The scorecard can weight such matters accordingly.

Numbers are important in grass-roots organisations and internet mailing lists are the most cost-effective method of volunteer communication. How effective such lists can be though is again a matter of deeper inquiry.

Activists are supporters who lack a public profile but are prepared to donate their time to your cause. Effective activists will also engage in viral campaigns, interact with the site and interact with other digital resources to improve your position.

Advocates, such as spokespersons and friendly journalists may not directly use any of your digital channels, but their presence and development of that presence in digital channels can be a useful internal metric for campaign development.

Example measures

Strategic Objective	Typical Measures	Example Digital metrics
Building Supporters	Passive membership Message adoption	E-mail list recipients Understanding of campaign message
Building Activists	Active membership Contribution	Postcard forwarding Attributed supporter sign-ups
Advocacy	Profile Popularity Personality	E-media presence Public support online Links to homepage

2.5 • Evolutionary perspective: extracting long-term value

➥ The Campaign against the Arms Trade is unlikely to win their case tomorrow. It is a political campaign with a long pedigree and potentially a long battle ahead. This is true of all but the most time-sensitive campaigning organisations.

Digital channels provide such organisations with a better understanding of their long-term position. Good businesses retain staff, good campaigns their active supporters.

Strong political entities are also diverse. Most political parties are coalitions of support and such affiliations can be mapped online. Content syndication is also a useful snap-shot of message proliferation.

Innovation in digital politics is often misunderstood and misused. It is not an innovation to be the first campaign to launch some whiz-bang application that business has been using for 3 years. Video-streaming your launch in 1999 was a nice headline but lousy cost management. True innovation can be either disruptive or evolutionary, but most importantly is persistent, understood and drives value.

Example measures

Strategic Objective	Typical Measures	Example Digital metrics
Enhancing core support	Supporter retention Intensity over time	% online renewing support Interactive usage patterns
Diversification	Partnering Participation	Affiliate grids Content contribution by site visitors
Innovation	Adoption	Effective deployment of new technology

Measuring digital campaigns

2.6 • Building a Political Research Architecture.

➥ So now you understand your campaign's strategic objectives and you can translate those objectives into targets for digital programmes. So what?

The next stage is to understand the way you campaign and build the research architecture that will inform the assessment of effectiveness and the achievement of campaign objectives.

2.61 • The Digital Campaign Cycle

The Digital Campaign Cycle is an approximation of the feedback loop that informs a rolling programme of campaigns.

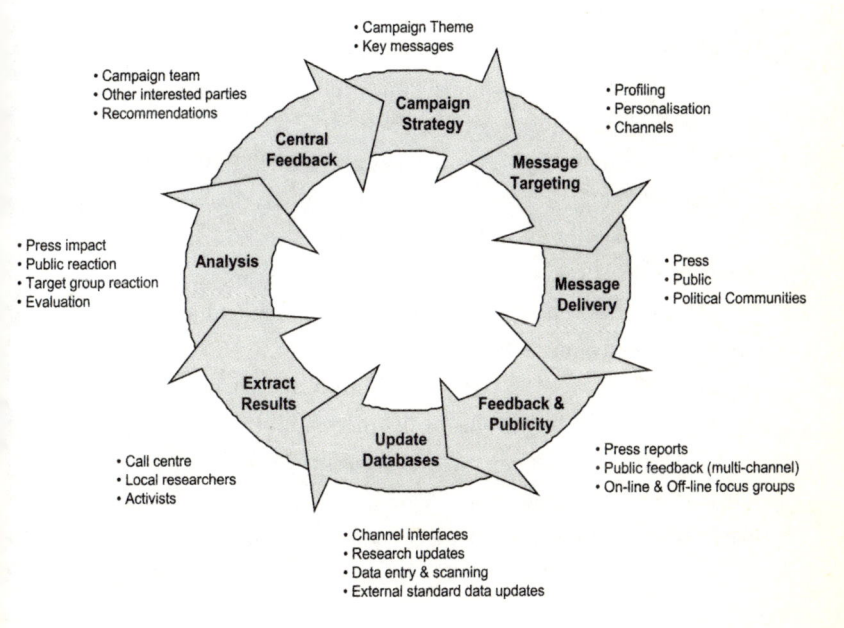

Campaign Strategy
- Campaign Theme
- Key messages

Message Targeting
- Profiling
- Personalisation
- Channels

Message Delivery
- Press
- Public
- Political Communities

Feedback & Publicity
- Press reports
- Public feedback (multi-channel)
- On-line & Off-line focus groups

Update Databases
- Channel interfaces
- Research updates
- Data entry & scanning
- External standard data updates

Extract Results
- Call centre
- Local researchers
- Activists

Analysis
- Press impact
- Public reaction
- Target group reaction
- Evaluation

Central Feedback
- Campaign team
- Other interested parties
- Recommendations

59

At each stage of the campaign cycle it is possible to apply a set of tools to evaluate progress against core metrics. These can then be understood as a set of programmes or products with reusable components.

2.6.2 • Strategic Research & Benchmarking

When embarking upon any type of activity that seeks to influence opinion, it is a pre-requisite that one understands to the fullest extent the situation as it stands before the activity commences. Whilst this may sound self-evident, an amazing number of communications initiatives of all sorts – commercial and political – start with only a rudimentary understanding of where they are starting from. This is surely like going on a diet without knowing what one's weight was on day one. You may end up with looser-fitting clothes and a good feeling about yourself, but you have no idea how much weight you have actually lost!

When it comes to digital media, many assume that things have to be done differently, simply because the medium is digital. In almost all cases this is a mistaken belief and it is certainly wrong when it comes to research. Firstly, one needs to ensure comparability with research findings generated in traditional ways and which relate to traditional media and secondly, the wheel simply does not need to be reinvented. It needs to be applied in a way that recognises the characteristics and limitations of the medium, but otherwise – for the most part – the principles remain the same.

In terms of benchmarking, there are certain consistent metrics that need to be understood across all groups researched:

- Current level of understanding of the issues
- Current opinion
- Current intentions (if applicable)
- Where they have been exposed to campaign messages
- How campaign leaders are viewed
- Expectations of the campaigning organisations
- Trust / credibility engendered by those organisations

In addition, one must also understand contextual factors that will help to assess the effectiveness and reach of different campaign activities:

- Access to and use of different media channels digital and otherwise
- Attitudes to technology
- Political viewpoint / loyalties
- Propensity to engage in political matters
  from voting at elections to volunteering for campaign activity

These factors will all help to deliver a deeper understanding of the effectiveness of a given campaign and its component parts. After all, unless one can segment research respondents in the most basic of ways, it is difficult to gain a clear picture of the results achieved. If one's sample base is disproportionately biased towards activists, one's interpretation of data can be significantly misleading and future campaigns can be based on erroneous assumptions.

This kind of benchmarking is of course dependent on being able to reach enough people within the different segments to be able to draw reliable conclusions. The approach most likely to yield returns

Viral Politics

is to conduct telephone research. Although more costly than online research, the latter will not deliver a sample that is representative of anything other than the user base of the sites or e-mail lists that are used to recruit. Whilst online research does have a role to play – not least in determining how users of the campaign site compare to the wider audience – it is not best suited to large scale benchmarking.

Naturally, cost issues raise their ugly heads at this point. Few campaigns are sufficiently well-financed to be able to justify diverting resources into large-scale research surveys, no matter how valuable the findings could be. The ideal world solution would be that such research be funded by a syndicate of political bodies with findings being shared by all as a planning, benchmarking and tracking resource (if repeated on a regular basis). Inevitably there would be compromise on issues addressed and pulling together such a group would be no easy matter, but bearing in mind cost-benefit factors, it could well be worth the effort.

In the absence of such collaboration, campaign managers are faced with either neglecting to benchmark at all or having to cobble together whatever they can from a range of other research measures such as focus groups, online surveys, small-scale telephone research and possibly face-to-face interviews. Pulling together and analysing data gathered using such diverse methodologies makes for less than ideal results with assumptions being less than robust, but in the absence of resource or collaboration, that is the reality faced by many.

2.6.3 • Technical Analysis
As is widely acknowledged in the digital media industries, the over-

reliance on technical data as a means of determining success has damaged the credibility of the medium. As such, it is something that is diminishing, to be replaced in part by more traditional measures.

Whilst things such as site traffic figures (page impressions, unique users, time spent on the site etc.) should not be ignored, they are by no means serious indicators of performance.

A page impression (i.e. one page downloaded by a user) tells you nothing about who downloaded it, what they took from it or how long they viewed it for – though the latter is available, it is seldom reported (often because the data is impenetrable to most people, but frequently because it doesn't make for palatable reading). Similarly, the number of unique users – although useful to indicate what might be driving traffic when it increases significantly following specific activity – tells us little or nothing about who is visiting and how they have been influenced. It is certainly a mistake to assume that what visitors take away from an interface – be it a web site or an e-mail – is what you intend them to take away.

Technical data in the form of log files should therefore be analysed for what it is: measures of volume. In the same way that we assess offline media targeting by not only how many people we reach, but also what type of people they are (demographics etc) we need to pursue a similar approach online.

2.6.4 • Message Tracking

Any campaign should understand its effectiveness in influencing attitudes held by target groups, but in the case of campaigns running over longer periods of time, there is the opportunity to assess impact as the campaign progresses and to develop the tactical approach taken accordingly.

This is where online polling can come into its own. As both a swift and cost-effective means of conducting research it scores highly. Using web site interfaces and e-mail lists to recruit respondents to participate in an online survey can quickly provide valuable insight to current opinion and what is driving it.

As previously mentioned, it is necessary to ask more than simply what people think on the issues at hand. We need to contextualise their answers by understanding something of their position in the first place, but this can be addressed in just a handful of questions.

There are basic guidelines to be followed when using online surveys that will elicit more responses in a shorter period of time. Firstly, surveys should be web-based rather than text based e-mails. If recruiting via e-mail lists, provide a link to the survey embedded in the text so that those wishing to respond can do so easily and those not interested can simply delete the e-mail. Web-based surveys will achieve better response rates than text based ones, partly because they are more appealing to the eye if well designed and partly because they can be much more mouse-driven for the respondent. Analysis of the many hundreds of surveys we have run shows clearly that whenever respondents are required to write an answer rather than click on an option, drop-out rates at that point in the survey escalate markedly.

Another advantage of web-based over e-mail-based surveys is the ability to route people around questions that are irrelevant to them on the basis of previous answers. There is frankly no excuse for a survey that contains something like "if the answer to question 7 is no, please go straight to question 10". Users don't like this and it is just bad practice that will negatively impact response rates and make the survey appear amateurish (not an impression you want associated with your campaign).

Similarly, survey writers should not succumb to the temptation to ask all the questions they would really love to have answers to. If a survey takes longer than four or five minutes to complete you will start to see significant uplift in drop-out rates and you will alienate those who started out as willing respondents – even if they do persevere and complete the survey. Incentives definitely help with online surveys, but the trick is to avoid incentives that bias responses by appealing to one group rather than another, or high value incentives for which people will be more likely to complete the survey just to get the reward rather than out of any interest in the subject. The consequence will be that they just tick boxes randomly giving you a large amount of ultimately misleading data.

The survey incentive that seems to work well is the chance to win something of moderate value that is easily used by many people – vouchers that are redeemable at online retailers such as Amazon are a pretty safe bet.

Naturally, if you are polling online, you should make sure that your questionnaire is as comparable as possible with any polling you are carrying out offline. Whilst the two should be analysed separately, together they will be more valuable if they are designed with reference to each other and it will become possible to identify differences between the offline and the online audiences which will help provide indicators as to relative performance of online and offline initiatives.

2.6.5 • Focus Groups

Focus Groups have suffered a bad press in recent years thanks to the perception that they have been over-used in the setting of policy by all parties. They are seen by many to represent the emphasis of message over content. However, properly conducted focus groups can offer a great deal to political campaigners seeking to optimise the impact of their work and to learn from each campaign undertaken.

As focus groups are so widely used in political research, it would be redundant to devote too much space to them here. There are a few valid points that should be made however, with regard to their use for campaign research and the principle benefits they offer at different stages.

2.6.5.1 • *Pre-campaign*: At this stage, the focus group can be most widely used to refine the campaign message and – more particularly – the way in which it is conveyed: tone of voice, specific executions etc. It is also a good time to research reaction to one's opponent's position and materials.

2.6.5.2 • *Mid-campaign:* As a form of qualitative tracking of public perception and response, focus groups are well established and can be very effective as a means of informing changes in tactics, response to events and modification of tone of voice. Due to the pace at which modern campaigns are run however, this approach is not always practical.

2.6.5.3 • *Post-campaign*: After a campaign the temptation is naturally to move on. However, to re-visit the subject shortly after its conclusion can yield valuable information for the next round or for different campaigns in the future. They are also a useful qualitative means of establishing just how much of the message has been assimilated and to what extent opinion may have been swayed in your favour (or otherwise) and what has driven this.

2.6.6 • Depth Interviews

In the context of campaign research, depth interviews serve much the same purpose as focus groups. They are best applied where the target respondents are unlikely to come together in a focus group or where the dynamic of a group discussion is not conducive to extracting honest opinion on the matter at hand – perhaps because of individual sensitivities.

In most cases, a structured programme of research amongst high-level opinion formers is likely to require the use of depth interviews which can be conducted either face-to-face or over the phone.

A secondary benefit of this approach is that the one-to-one dialogue can also have a positive effect on the relationship with respondents. It is always flattering to be asked for one's opinion no matter who you are, especially if you feel it will influence people's thinking. However, it is important that the research agenda does not take second place to a relationship-building exercise. This will almost certainly be spotted by respondents and the value of the research itself will be compromised.

2.7 • Developing the Research Architecture

➡ Each campaign is likely to require a different research architecture. Similarly, each campaign has to work within different constraints of manpower, funding, time, and so on. It is therefore meaningless to attempt to prescribe a 'one size fits all' approach to defining the optimum research architecture for digital political campaigning per se.

Campaign managers can be best served by integrating the evaluation process into the earliest stages of campaign planning by adopting the political scorecard approach in order to then define not only what should be measured, but also how the best measurement can be achieved within the operational constraints that are faced.

We have outlined some of the methodologies that are most likely to yield meaningful results, but perhaps the most important thing to bear in mind when addressing the issue of campaign research is that of consistency.

One of the core benefits of a properly defined research architecture is that it effectively identifies the right components for the campaign at hand and it almost forces their consistent application and analysis of findings.

Over time, using the results of your research programme it will become clear which of your core objectives are being met, which are persistently below par and which yield no useful information.

They will encourage you to build measurement into your digital programmes and not be fobbed off with advice to experiment without clear expectations of delivery. For example, if an SMS campaign is delivering hits, but negative mindshare and high costs, it can be assessed, then amended or dropped rather than continued because it is seen as the most innovative activity of its kind.

If a banner advert is frequently viewed, but only boosts public support for your opponent's views, it too can be altered.

The key is building the expectation of outcomes into the digital campaign before, not during or after the event.

Likewise if a particular technique – for example on-line forums – cannot be made to fit any of your core objectives in a measurable fashion, it is probably not worth doing.

This, we believe, is the way digital campaigns will be assessed in the future. Not all campaigns will be able to assess activity to the fullest extent as we do not live in an ideal world. This approach is only now starting to gain ground in the commercial sector, where resources are more readily available and where accountability – at least within large companies – is embedded in the culture.

However this does mean, that those who are willing and able to pursue such a structured and rigorous approach will achieve competitive advantage by doing little more than what should be considered basic best practice.

2.6.8 • Conclusion

➡ Using a structured research architecture informed by strategic intent is vital to building better digital campaigns. Using even simple

Viral Politics

metrics can lead to a better understanding of both the technology and the whys, whos, and hows, it can work.

Below, we have given an example of a campaign and its judgements about effective communications channels for promotion of the campaign's objectives – judgements made through research. The campaign had two objectives: to better target their channels and better target their core digital functions according to the needs of key stakeholders. A combination of techniques were used at the strategic stage of the campaign and the results were justified against actual usage of delivered techniques as the campaign evolved.

Routes to Targets

● - Highly Effective or preferred communication channel
◐ - Secondary communication channel
○ - Usually ineffective or not preferred

Channel Targeting - What works best with who

Target Group	Direct Mail (GPO)	Telephone	Fax	Pager	SMS	Text e-mail	Rch Media e-mail	Written Requests	Phone Requests	Fax Requests	e-mail	PC Internet	PC Intranet	PC Extranet	Mobile Internet	Mobile Extranet	Web TV	Print News	TV News	Advertising	Leafleting	Canvassing	Digital TV
Press	○	●	●	○	○	○	○	○	●	●	○	○	○	●	○	○	○	○	○	○	○	○	○
Spokespersons	○	●	●	●	○	○	○	○	●	●	●	○	●	●	○	●	○	○	○	○	○	○	○
Benefactors	●	●	○	○	○	○	○	◐	○	○	◐	○	○	○	○	○	○	○	○	○	○	○	○
Supporters	●	●	○	○	○	●	○	●	●	○	●	●	○	○	○	○	○	◐	●	○	○	○	○
Voters	●	◐	○	○	○	○	○	○	○	○	○	●	○	○	○	○	●	●	●	○	○	●	○

Functionality Targeting

- ● - Highly Relevant, push information
- ◐ - For information only
- ○ - Little or no relevance

Target Group	Message Delivery						Datasets									Digital Features												
	Press Releases	Speeches	Articles	Lines to take	Features	Membership data	Voter (canvassing reutnrs)	Sociogrphaic research	Policy research	Press Contacts	Press Archive	Campaigns archives	Donation history	Recruitment forms	Donation form	Customer call-back & support	Party shop	Webmail	Local homepages	e-cards (e-mail a friend)	e-groups (mailing lists/newsletters)	Polls & passive research	e-focus groups and active research	Audio Streaming	Video Streaming	Unified Messaging (fax/e-mail/voice)
Press	●	●	○	○	●	○	○	○	○	●	○	○	○	○	●	○	○	○	○	○	○	○	○	●	●	●
Spokespersons	●	●	●	●	○	○	○	○	●	○	○	○	○	○	○	◐	○	◐	●	○	○	◐	○	○	○	●
Supporters (Volunteers)	○	○	●	●	○	●	○	○	○	○	●	●	○	○	○	●	○	●	●	●	●	●	●	○	○	●
Supporters (Staff)	●	○	○	●	○	●	●	●	●	●	●	●	●	○	○	●	○	●	●	●	●	●	●	○	○	●
Benefactors	○	○	○	●	○	○	○	○	○	○	○	○	○	◐	●	●	○	○	○	○	○	○	○	○	○	◐
Voters	○	○	○	○	○	○	○	○	○	○	○	○	○	●	●	●	◐	◐	○	●	◐	●	●	●	●	●

This is not a campaign that would have expended much effort SMS'ing the party shop URL to key Benefactors on their WAP phones.

Good digital campaign research is not a slave to technology, it applies technology to the needs the campaign and sets an objective basis for measurement. If digital campaigners and their organisations can learn from these techniques then many of the wasteful errors that have sunk commercial digital propositions can be avoided.

3.

How e-democracy can help deliver better public services

Stephan Shakespeare, co-founder of YouGov.com[1]

➦ Over the last few hundred years, there has been a huge increase in the scope of government, and yet very little development in the fundamental basis of democracy – voting. British governments, suspicious of referenda, prefer opinion polling and focus groups as additional ways to connect to the views of the public. Useful as this approach may be to government, it does little for citizens as they have no sense of being involved. It confers all the power on government, which can choose to respond or ignore mere opinion polls.

However, the Labour Government has also taken the democratic agenda forward by introducing 'stakeholder consultation'. Local and regional government, as well as services such as the NHS and the Police, must now consult with stakeholders (that is, people with a vested interest in the organisation either as participants or receivers of services) prior to making strategic decisions. This has the potential for empowering citizens without moving to 'direct democracy'.

Although there have been excellent examples of thorough and helpful consultation exercises which have led to policy improvements, the fact is that most have tended to involve very few citizens, and the process has too often been seen as frustrating by the consultees, and obstructive or time-wasting by the consultors. Most people lead busy lives and are not necessarily keen to turn up at meetings in Town Halls, nor to fill in questionnaires. A recent attempt by a city to consult residents on whether they wanted an executive mayor cost hundreds of thousands of pounds and yielded 87 responses. Another consultation, by an NHS Health Authority, cost tens of thousands and ended up with five members of the public attending a meeting. It was written up as a great success.

The consultors tend to see this process as obstructive because it is both time consuming, and tends to attract involvement only from those with an axe to grind. To be successful, consultation needs to reach a critical level of public engagement. Fortunately, the opportunities offered by the internet allow for a much more interactive and constructive form of consultation – easy for large numbers of stakeholders to engage in, quick, and producing rich, useful and authoritative data.

Before considering how e-consultation can improve the actual delivery of services, we must first consider the legitimacy of the internet as a way of measuring opinions.

3.1 • Internet versus conventional polling

When ICM pioneered telephone based interviews for opinion polling in the UK, there was considerable resistance; it was perceived as biased, as not everyone was available on the telephone. In the past eleven years, telephone polling has not only become routine, it has become a preferred method, as it has the advantage of speed and cost efficiency. Furthermore, many people have become reluctant to engage in face-to-face interviews. This reluctance leads to sample skew: people with views they don't care to share with an interviewer de-select themselves from the sample, as do those with little time to spare. Non-response is acknowledged by the market research industry as the single largest problem facing it.

Just as telephone polls had to prove their validity in the eighties, the internet must do so now. While the internet community can be weighted to yield exactly the same demographic and opinion profile as the UK as a whole, other forms of skew might intrude – are the 40 per cent of the population who are Internet users different from the other 60 per cent? In some respects, clearly yes. But the evidence suggests that for most forms of opinion research, there is no reason to see these groups as significantly different. Indeed, internet polling has demonstrably made a good start: at the last US Presidential elections, the exclusively internet-based polling company Harris Interactive produced among the closest predictions of the actual result. In the British general election last June, an online panel of over 7,000 people (conducted by YouGov for the British Election Survey / the Economic and Social Research Council) produced the closest result of all the opinion pollsters.

Possible disadvantages of internet polling are counteracted by strong advantages. Not only can large samples be recruited quickly and surveys processed almost instantly, but internet polling methodology allows for much richer data. Online panels allow researchers to return to respondents as often as necessary, either with new topics or variations on previous questions, to tease out complex background detail on attitudes and opinions, and lead to dynamic 'negotiated solutions'. This allows us to fill the enormous gap between the two extremes of current methodologies – that is, between focus groups (yielding rich qualitative data which cannot be quantitatively measured) and conventional opinions polls (yielding objectively measurable but narrow and shallow data). Data extracted from internet polling is extremely rich and deep, and objectively measurable. With the large numbers of respondents available it is possible to adjust for sample skew.

All methods of opinion research have their problems, and there is rarely a simple 'right answer' when choosing between them. A comparison of internet and conventional polling methodologies can be summarised as follows:

1 internet polling is faster: it can supply results within hours of the survey being agreed
2 internet polling allows for richer presentation than conventional polling: rich visual and audio content can be presented, and questions can be longer and more complex, as they are presented on-screen
3 internet polling allows for more options, including taking respondents through different sub-surveys
4 internet polling is more flexible: interim results can allow

one quickly to assess results and modify the poll if necessary
5   internet panel-based polling allows for much richer data, as responses from previous surveys can be cross-referenced with responses from the current survey, showing actual change of opinion as well as correlating data across disparate topics
6   internet panel-based polling allows 'drilling down' into views and 'negotiating solutions' by returning to respondents with differentiated follow-up surveys as necessary
7   internet polling allows for easier recruitment of specialist panels – for example by recruiting from specialist websites or by selecting from very large samples
8   internet polling is more 'frank and honest' – evidence suggests that people are more willing to give their true views to a machine than to fellow humans
9   on the negative side, internet polling is restricted to respondents who are online. However, if numbers are large enough then it is easy to create a panel that reflects any required demographic profile. Evidence suggests that internet users are not different from non-internet users in their opinions on non-technology-related issues.

3.2 • Consultation versus opinion polling

➥   If opinion polling is the science of evaluating the views of a representative sample of a defined group (whether the UK population or, say, women in Yorkshire), consultation is about providing a platform for anyone who wants to have their say. If a council (for example) seeks the views of its citizens on an issue, an opinion poll may accurately report a cross-section of opinion (albeit on a narrow base of questions which have been defined by the council); however, individual citizens will have no sense of having been personally involved. Therefore, they feel no ownership of the process by which decisions are made. To put it negatively: opinion polling can too easily become an instrument to aid effective manipulation, while real, open consultation is an essential element of democracy. But, as we have already noted, most of the current consultation exercises have been disappointing, because too few – and untypical – citizens have been involved. We need to look again at how to make consultation easy and engaging. People need to feel that they can get involved without inconvenience, and that the process will actually make a difference.

3.3 • E-consultation: a new model

➡ Internet-based consultation offers six advantages over the conventional process (which of course should be seen as running in tandem; consultation, for obvious reasons, must always allow for off-line responses; the internet offers an additional channel, not an exclusive one):

1. Internet-based consultation is easy. People who have access to the internet can participate in minutes.
2. By advertising nationally that there is a 'UK Consults' panel open to all, potential respondents can be e-mailed as needed for separate consultations. People can feel able to interact with government or service-providers on a continuous basis.
3. Internet-based consultation is empowering: respondents can feel awed by having to express themselves directly to professionals or politicians; internet users are comfortable responding on the internet in a mistake-free environment.
4. Internet-based consultation is cost-effective compared to offline processes.
5. The consultation can be deliberative and complex. At the same time it can be simple for the participant. Moreover, by using the 'negotiated solution' approach, in which interaction continues, a realistic conclusion is reached.
6. Internet-based consultation can address the issue of who has control of the consultation. While a genuinely democratic model will take time to develop, in the future one would imagine a genuinely interactive, open, shared-responsibility model, in which:

    a The survey should ask respondents: 'Do you feel the right questions have been asked? What other questions should be asked? (e-mail responses)' This reduces the sense that those in power are in control of the questions.

An independent arbiter should decide which further questions should be put.

b The survey should ask respondents: 'Do you feel you have the information you need to answer these or other questions? What other information should be provided? (e-mail responses)' An independent arbiter should decide which further information should be provided.

c Respondents should be sent a copy of the results and final report.

d Respondents should be informed (by an independent arbiter) to what use the results are being put. Has the consultation resulted in the views of citizens being implemented? If not, why not?

3.3.1 • Who benefits?

If government consults openly and non-manipulatively with citizens, then both parties benefit. If government acts on the consultation, then citizens share the responsibility for what happens. Citizens are more likely to understand the difficult choices being faced; they are more likely to get their needs addressed, in the context of what is realistic. Government can be more confident in its actions; it can truly say it is serving the people, not exploiting them for power. Through effective, interactive and widespread consultation, citizens and government work together to improve society at the detailed, everyday level, and also holistically.

The commercial sector can reap the same benefits. Getting

'close to the customer' is already a central aim of most businesses. The ultimate aim of a business is to make profits, while the aim of customers is to get the best for their money. Conventional market research exists to bring those aims together. But businesses and customers operate in a society: citizens and their government (as opposed to the business or the customer) stand over both. Increasing importance is placed on 'corporate social responsibility'. Governments are more sympathetic to businesses that are responsive to all stakeholders. The more businesses, customers, citizens and government understand each other, the more successful the outcome for all of them.

The process of consultation should be carried out at arm's length from the government. Consultation is not a referendum. We elect a government to manage for a given period. It has the responsibility for providing leadership and making decisions. Citizens are the ultimate arbiters only on election day.

The government must reserve the right to ignore all or part of the results of a consultation – so long as it is open about it. If it carries out the equivalent of 'official opinion polls', it is restricted in its ability to manage according to its convictions.

3.4 • Improving Public Services by e-consultation

➡ Having discussed the legitimacy of the internet as a tool for opinion research and consultation, we now return to our main theme: how can this process actually help to make our lives better in a practical way? Democracy is a fine thing, but will it make the trains run on time?

The issue is not just how to give the people a voice, but how to make them take responsibility in equal measure. To use the phrase of Matthew Taylor (of the Institute of Public Policy Research): 'how do we implicate the public in the decision-making process?'

And then to take it one step further: how can the digital revolution change democratic relationships in a way that makes the daily lives of citizens more pleasant, healthier, more productive and fulfilling?

The relationship between democracy and delivery of public services was the real theme of the general election we have just had. The best explanation for low voter turn-out was low enthusiasm for what the public perceived as a political process forever making promises but never quite fulfilling them.

So, how can the digital revolution transform public services?

There is a direct and strong link between philosophical issues and the practical outcomes that we all seek. It is based on the relationships within the system that drive outcomes. The way we run our public services is juvenile. I use the word carefully, and not abusively, as an ex-teacher and a parent. In the world of education, the real, lasting break-throughs in the classroom (and the home) come when children realise that the work they are doing is for their own future. Until that moment, they believe that manipulating and fighting the teacher – or alternatively buckling down to do as they are told – is the main purpose of life. After they have understood and internalised that there is a connection between what they do and how their own lives will turn out, they treat the teacher as a facilitator and become self-motivated.

In schools, this generally happens (if it happens at all) between the ages of 14 to 18. However, the power relationships within public services – and indeed many parts of the commercial sector too – are institutionalised in a way that ensures we never reach the desired state of mature self-motivation and team-work. As a result, organisations such as the NHS are as inefficient and self-defeating as an unruly classroom of twelve-year-olds, ruled over by an exhausted teacher.

Doctors, nurses, unions and the general public all behave like children blaming the teacher (or their parents) for the misery of their lives. The government is the boss, making unfair rules, demanding unreasonable work, and not doling out enough pocket-money. Doctors, nurses, unions and the general public unite in bewailing the awfulness of the boss. Meanwhile the boss feels hurt and confused (he is only trying to do his best), and alternates between speaking smoothly to calm the chaos, and lashing out in frustration.

How do we create the team-work which is the only possible solution to this failure of the system?

Digital democracy can help. By carrying out consultations online, people can engage quickly, when and where it suits them. A small incentive can compensate people for the short period of time it takes to get involved and they can participate in the comfort of their homes or offices, and when it is convenient to them. Experience has shown that significant databases can be built-up relatively quickly. If you have a database of at least 10,000 people, sample skew is not an issue: with such large numbers, all the demographic segments can be well represented. While the process may be quick and easy, it also allows for great complexity, because you can return to respondents again and again to tease out the vital underlying detail and motivations of their views, present new information, and arrive at 'negotiated solutions' to issues. This contrasts with the extremely superficial nature of the data obtained by conventional opinion polls, and the rich but subjective data obtained by focus groups.

Furthermore, the process is 'sticky' – people stay with it. Once they take part, they generally want to continue to take part. In a recent survey, 37 per cent cited 'payment' as the main reason for engaging in e-consultation, but 53 per cent cited 'taking part in democracy'. The advantage of consultation via an open platform, as opposed to opinion polling, is that if the process is advertised then everyone feels they have been invited; while opinion polls randomly select a few.

But however efficient and satisfying we can make this form of consultation, and however much it may enhance the conventional off-line process, it does not address the second, deeper issue: the structure of the stakeholder relationships.

Here it is necessary to return to the 'juvenile' nature of those relationships, the teacher-to-pupil, parent-to-child, boss-to-worker power structures. The client agency poses the questions to its stakeholders. The respondent is asked, in essence: 'What do you want?' Satisfaction, although only in the short-term, will follow according to how much the agency can fulfil the demand. However open the process, this reinforces responsibility for the agency, and irresponsibility for the respondent.

Such a consultation process gives the client an interesting array of data, but it doesn't solve the problem. Now he knows what the competing demands of his stakeholders are, but does that help him to juggle them any better? What is needed is a consultation process that changes the nature of all the relationships from antagonistic to co-operative. A linear process, with the client as the centre of a series of single relationships, cannot do that.

Take the case of the National Health Service: we know that the government cannot fulfill all the competing demands made on it. In fact, the government can only give money and make organisational rules; this is not the same. The real demand for a better service can only be fulfilled by doctors, nurses, managers, unions and patients, working together as a team.

But the structure of the current health debate makes that impossible. Doctors, represented by the British Medical Association, attack the government on pay. Nurses, represented by the Royal College of Nursing, attack the government on pay and conditions. Ancillary staff, represented by Unison, attack the government on pay and job security. The pressure from patients is for better service, more treatments, cleaner hospitals and expensive drugs.

What can the government do? It is faced with unmanageable contradictions: the demands of doctors, nurses, ancillary staff, and patients are completely out of harmony. For example, my four-year-old daughter lost four days just as she was settling in to her first school, so that she could be in hospital for just two hours of tests. Why? Because the hospital couldn't be sure when the consultant would be popping in. As a patient, my complaint may be against the working practices of doctors, but I am most likely to express it as a complaint against the government over lack of resources.

So the government finds itself blamed for everything, but unable to get a grip on the situation, and like the teacher in a chaotic classroom, alternates between trying to calm the situation with soothing words, or shouting back in anger.

But the government must also blame itself. By always putting itself in the centre of the circle, with its stakeholder relationships radiating like spokes of a wheel, it takes on the position of controller. But it cannot possibly control everything successfully. In fact, all it can really control is the money – which it takes from the most powerful stakeholder group: the tax-payer. The more it tries to control, the more it removes responsibility from everyone else.

Government becomes the focus of all debate, whether or not the solution lies there. The government can take more from the tax-payer and feed it into the system. The tax-payer may be willing, but only if guaranteed results. But the government cannot guarantee anything without team-work from all the stakeholders.

To deliver a better NHS, the stakeholders must work together, understand each other, come to compromises directly between each other, not always mediated by the government. Doctors, nurses, cleaners, managers, unions, patients and taxpayers must talk together and work out joint solutions. Then they will all be implicated in the delivery of a better NHS.

It requires a major shift in how the government perceives its role. Of course it cannot relinquish its position as the ultimate guarantor and referee of the system; we do not have (and probably do not want) direct democracy with referenda on all decisions. But the government will have to change the stakeholder map: no longer seeing itself always at the centre of the circle, it must give up total control and total responsibility; it must stop taking all the credit or blame. The key job of the government is to provide reliable funds and be a back-stop regulator to avert disaster. Let the system start taking responsibility for itself.

For example, we all know that we have health rationing. Whether through the National Institute of Clinical Excellence (which decides which treatments are cost-effective – in other words, what the NHS can afford), or through unspoken agreement between doctors as to who is worth treating and who is not, we deal with shortages by not telling the public. Imagine instead we asked the public directly: which treatments are you prepared to fund, and for whom?

It would be a simple question, but setting off a complex mental process for all who participated. Instead of simply blaming the government for the 'lack of resources', people would suddenly find themselves having to resolve their own convenient schizophrenia, bringing together the public-as-patients and the public-as-tax-payers.

Once that dangerous split is confronted – merely in the act of answering an open and difficult question – other issues would also naturally demand resolution. When we make choices, not as voters looking to government for blame and fulfillment but as members of equal stakeholder groups communicating with each other, then we begin to ask each other the right questions. The patient talks to the nurse, the doctor, and the cleaner and says, 'if I pay you more, what will you do for me?'

That is the real advantage of the private sector. It is not the profit-motive as a base driver of efficiency, but the open exchange of money creating an honest deal. In a private hospital, the individual patient actually matters to the doctor, the nurse, the cleaner and the manager, because their income depends on the customer's payment. Which is why in a private hospital the doctors, nurses, cleaners and managers actually talk to each other, listen to each other, and take quick action to make things work better, in contrast to an NHS hospital, where institutionalised resistance means no-one bothers.

This is not an appeal for the privatisation of the NHS. The taxpayer doesn't want that. This is an appeal to get the same inter-stakeholder dialogue – and resulting action – in the public sector as we see more often in the private sector.

We can do it without money changing hands. To repeat, the essence of the process is inter-stakeholder dialogue. But this is not about committee meetings. For it to work, inter-stakeholder dialogue must be dynamic, open and above all broad-based. Everyone must either take part, or know they could have taken part quickly and easily if they had wanted to. And here, finally, we come back to digital democracy.

We have all kinds of dialogue. The most valuable is between two or three people. But colossal national systems – like the health, the education, and the police services – cannot be resolved by informal human interactions. Formal, broadly-based human interactions, such as might occur at elections or large-scale consultation meetings, are too cumbersome and tend to be obstructive to actually running services. The only way to have mass inter-stakeholder dialogue which is both formal and dynamic is online.

And in this form, the process becomes remarkably simple. Build your online panel – ideally it should be a huge number, but what really matters is that everyone knows they can join in – and you can manage the consultation as easily as if you were dealing with just a handful in a room. In fact, more easily: we know from experience that respondents are frank and more likely to be 'reasonable' than when arguing in a room. This does not require a vast technological superstructure, nor even complex management.

The important thing is that it is not the government which is asking the questions. There are too many questions which government simply cannot ask, for fear of getting the wrong answer. Once it has asked a question, how can it ignore the response? But it is not, in the first place, for the government to respond; it is for the other stakeholders.

If government controls the stakeholder dialogue, it will be fruitless, simply pumping up demands which cannot be met.[2]

In effect, the stakeholder groups are putting questions to each other, and responding to each other. They are not in dialogue with the Government, they are building a team-work approach to the service.

What is incredibly difficult to organise in a conventional stakeholder consultation is now possible in the online form. One of the great strengths of the internet is that it can make complexity easy. Specifically in the area of opinion research, many different kinds of questions can be put to many sub-sections of the audience, building up a map of opinion that matches the true variety and interdependence of real dialogue.

It is essential that the government commissions the process and supports implementation, but it cannot take control, otherwise it re-establishes the very power-relationships which have distorted the debate and led to the inefficiencies in the system.

Government must understand how little it is trusted. In research carried out recently we discovered that the Department of Health was the least trusted partner of the NHS, significantly below even the pharmaceutical industry. Furthermore, the government is seen as the source of the resources which, in a centralised dialogue, become the answer to every problem. This is a powerful combination which creates a significant barrier to progress. That is why the process needs a disinterested third party to make it work.[3]

The problem is simply this: getting people to do what is in their own best interests. But merely telling people that the way they are living their lives or doing business is wrong does nothing to make them change; if anything, it increases their resistance. Remember: they tend to distrust and dislike government. London Remade, a new kind of recycling project owned by the Association of London Government, The Greater London Authority, and London First, is taking this new approach through mass stakeholder consultation. It has already established an online panel of 3,000 Londoners, segmented into different stakeholder groups. That is just the pilot for a strategy to develop a panel of over 100,000. With the help of the Department for Education, all London's school children will get involved online, learning about the issues then interviewing their parents at home, reporting back on the Internet, and thereby dragging another million Londoners into the process.

Londoners should discover how to solve the problems of mounting rubbish for themselves, and that means informed inter-stakeholder dialogue. If the pilot is effective it is hoped that a means by which a step-increase in the quantity of our recycling can be devised – a means that is practical, convenient and even profitable.

Working online means that it is no more cumbersome to involve a million than a hundred people. That is the essence of how this tool can serve democracy: you can have a genuine, dynamic conversation which produces inter-stakeholder negotiated solutions to the problems which government, with its top-down structures, can never even contemplate.

So the challenge of engagement, which nearly all politicians are now discussing, becomes much easier. Instead of trying to get people involved in a thousand different meetings – which we all know will never happen – simply give them an opportunity, and an incentive, to join an online panel. From that point on, the process develops its own life. We are already seeing the process beginning in a range of pilots. The only thing that stands between taking these pilots from isolated but interesting experiments to a new way of doing democracy, is the willingness of government to hand over more control to its people. In doing so, it will find the solution to what has come to be seen as the intractable problem of our public services.

Notes

[1] YouGov Opinion Research, partner of Freeserve and the Economic and Social Research Council for the British Election Survey, has established itself as the leading UK Internet Polling and e-consultation company.

[2] YouGov is already beginning to experiment with this and building an online panel for an NHS health authority and a police authority, and we are designing a structure for training (bringing together pupils, educators and trainers, and businesses). We begin by asking a series of questions which tease out the views of each stakeholder group. Many questions will overlap between groups, others will be specific to them. Once the initial views of the groups are known, we put a second survey to each group, or sub-groups (as appropriate).

[3] Our biggest pilot of this approach is for London Remade, a new kind of recycling project (owned by the Association of London Government, the Greater London Authority, and London First) which is getting residents, businesses, local government, entrepreneurs, and environmentalists to work

together in a complex way. We know how to reduce our reliance on landfill, how to increase by huge multiples our present level of recycling, and how to do it in a way that is practical, convenient and even profitable.

4.

Unified message, many channels

Introducing a 'New Hal' for the 21st Century

Ben Wardle

➡ *Hal has been re-branded for his coming of age. Old Hal (the megalomaniac computer in Arthur C Clarke's book '2001: A Space Odyssey' and eponymous film) is no longer fit to be a metaphor for a space odyssey, let alone a political one. Arthur C Clarke's scary computer with a mind of its own just isn't savvy enough any more, he just doesn't understand that the needs of his audience have changed. Advertising execs, pollsters and a new breed of political hacks have decided that Hal is no longer able to meet the needs and aspirations of the voting public.*

With a new visual identity and no ideological baggage, they are set to unveil 'New Hal' (though there is some debate as to whether or not there should be a capital 'n' for 'new').

New Hal's neural architecture allows him to adapt and learn from success and failure. He can analyse why something has happened and change his own programming to recreate or avoid such an event. It may take him a couple of elections to get up and running – it's a steep learning curve to turn yourself into the ultimate political machine.

New Hal can even operate his own call centres and tele-canvassing banks, making and receiving thousands of calls simultaneously.

Since New Hal 1.54 (known as the 'Bobby' release), he has been able to track polls, make policy, write speeches and Party Election Broadcasts. New Hal creates his own content for every distribution channel that can be accessed electronically.

New Hal 2.01 can save politicians time and effort – he just plugs straight into the networks and creates virtual appearances by party leaders and candidates. He can even manage and create celebrities to connect with individual audiences. The 'Des O'Connor' module is a particular success amongst key swing voters.

New Hal is an integrated political machine, designed to win elections. There has been much criticism of political parties for not using new technologies to empower citizens, but to deliver propaganda designed to win votes instead. New Hal makes no silicon bones about being nothing more than a party animal. New technologies can be used to empower ordinary citizens, but the key thing is that the technology allows them to do it themselves – to mobilise interest groups based on communities of geography, interest and demography. New Hal would engage with these new online interest groups, but would not seek to facilitate them rather like his off-line equivalent.

Unified Message, many channels

4.1 • Party politics in many places at one time.

➥ New Hal may be your dystopia or utopia (probably depending on whether or not at the end of the day it's your hand that hovers over the reset button). New Hal was born, ironically, after the consumption of a large quantity of a beer called Freedom in one of George Orwell's old stomping grounds. All computers are equal, but some are more equal than others. There are, however, interesting and serious points that can be drawn from New Hal.

New Hal offers us a practical mantra – the three priorities of integration, integration and integration. Political parties are sprawling beasts, with often unconnected databases of members, supporters, donors, activists and the public at large. Such data is held at a number of levels, both nationally and locally, and includes voters contact information from phones, doorstep canvassing and e-mail. Sophisticated ICT can integrate these datasets to allow party activists and officials to make more informed decisions.

Call centres should be able to bring up voting intentions and every other piece of relevant information that has been gleaned about a caller who rings the party. Imagine a situation where the party representative who is making the call knows that someone has accessed the party website three times within the past fortnight, has registered online as a floating voter and spent their time browsing education policy. The calling scripts can be tailored so that the voter will receive a highly personalised telephone call rather than just the usual generalities.

Voting intentions volunteered online should be seamlessly integrated into the data that activists have available when banging on doors to get out the vote on polling day.

The ability to narrowcast messages to highly targeted audiences is one of the greatest benefits of new technologies. Political parties and campaigning organisations need to be able to adopt the same techniques used by successful e-commerce operations. At Amazon, the site adapts to your preferences, learning the particular genres and formats you are interested in. Even if you are not a regular or registered user of the site, it will suggest books bought by other users that purchased the same book you are browsing.

Sophisticated travel sites know from your previous searches, itineraries and purchases that you may have a penchant for designer hotels in big US cities or just like to book cheap European flights. They then tailor your browsing experience in a seamless fashion to suit your needs and interests. Yes, it is designed to sell more products, but online consumers are an increasingly savvy bunch and visit such sites because they don't need to spend hours searching for things they might want to buy. Personalisation can create a much more satisfying and efficient user experience, meeting the needs of both consumer and retailer.

Annanova, the online news service established by the Press Association and sold to Orange/France Telecom, features an 'update' button on every story. This allows site visitors to be kept informed of relevant breaking news by e-mail or mobile phone text message, selected by a series of topics or keywords. Even the simple use of 'cookies' (a small file that stores information about you so that the web-site can respond to your individual preferences when you return to the site) to allow you to store your channel preferences in its TV listings is a highly effective way of keeping you loyal, and it doesn't ask for your e-mail address either. Campaigning sites should follow suit in their ability to 'push' information to users who have 'opted in' to receive it.

At the risk of sounding like an advertorial here, Annanova also offers a mix of light-hearted stories as well as serious content which often make it a far more engaging casual read than BBC News. A little more 'human interest' and humour on party sites could create a far more appealing package. There are other lessons here though – Annanova invested heavily in a 'virtual newsreader' which, as a marketing gimmick, has proved to be a mildly effective vehicle, but, comes across as slightly superfluous even on a broadband connection.

Online campaigns should be wary about spending through the nose to create online gimmicks that will please only a few advertising executives and the web developers. The newsreader does however allow you to make decisions about the type of news you would like to view after each story – something that parties could consider in their video streaming plans.

Like 'New Hal', online campaigns will need to evolve and learn. Regular online feedback, usability polls and tests should be conducted to find out how campaigns can best meet the needs and expectations of visitors. Designs and navigation need to be thoroughly run through focus groups and assessments made of usability. The American Liberty Foundation, a libertarian think tank, has gained much publicity by asking visitors to its website to help create its new television ad campaign.

The public will expect political parties to provide the same technological quality online as they expect of commercial and entertainment sites. This means providing quality audio and video broadcasts as well as interesting and compelling words and pictures. Not just broadcasting their press conferences and the occasional speech, but filming and packaging a regular stream of interviews, news broadcasts and local content in a wide variety of formats.

The type of content suitable for viewing on a broadband connected PC (that is a PC with high speed internet access) may not be very different technically from that which would be streamed to a third generation (3G) mobile phone (which will also have a high-speed internet connection), but in terms of length and content it may need to be very different. Those using their PC may want to watch a longer campaign film, but those using 3G may prefer a 15 second clip – possibly pushed as a Multimedia Message. Long distance shots may help provide atmosphere on widescreen TV, but are likely to just cause confusion on a mobile phone or PDA (handheld device) screen.

Investment will need to be made in equipment and personnel to allow local candidates to produce their own broadcasts and allow 'roving' cameras to follow national figures on their travels. A veritable army of camera operators, editors and producers could be needed.

4.2 • Politics on the go

➥ Mobile phone usage in the UK and Europe is quite different to that in the US. The US still has a much greater density of internet than mobile penetration, while the situation is reversed in Western Europe. A study by Carl H Marcusson of Denmark's Bornholm Research Centre found a mobile phone density of 62 per cent in Western Europe at the end of 2000. This figure was just 40 per cent at the end of 1999 and 24 per cent the previous year. Around one in ten phones are not actively used however and some people use more than one handset. Marcusson estimates that around fifty per cent of the population are making active use of mobile phones. In comparison 27 per cent have access to the web and just 1.7 per cent make use of WAP connectivity.

By 2003 Marcusson predicts that mobile density in Western Europe will be up to 97 percent, however there will be an increased use of multiple handsets by individuals and the inactivity rate will increase too, so around two thirds of the population will own and use phones. In comparison, 39 per cent of the European population will have web access and 16 percent will make some use of WAP enabled phones.

At the end of 2000, 12 per cent of the world population had mobile phones, whereas just 7 per cent had access to the web. Analysts at Dresdner Kleinwort Benson feel phone ownership growth is reaching its inflexion point in Europe, beyond which further growth will be restrained.

JD Power and Associates have estimated that in the UK just 10 per cent of mobiles are WAP capable and less than one in three of these have ever been used for WAP access. With such a low density of WAP take up, the reality is that online campaigns shouldn't invest too much time or money on delivering content using WAP, but ought to have a minimal presence. Perhaps usage will increase if WAP set-up becomes more user friendly (even for those who are technologically savvy, WAP can be cumbersome and fiddly to set up), but reading a few words of information at a time is not a very satisfying experience and there are many WAP gateway issues that make delivering more rich content tricky.

New mobile technologies such as Multimedia Messaging (MMS) will soon come on stream allowing rich audio and video content to be attached to text messages. We won't have to wait until 3G finally emerges, as the interim upgrade to existing networks (known as GPRS) provides 15 times greater speeds than existing systems and a 'data always on' facility.

Nokia has already unveiled its new standard for MMS, dubbed Artuse. The market leading mobile handset has created development and server environments to allow third party software developers to get to grips with the new technology before it becomes available to the mass market. Nokia's Mobile Entertainment Services division has also formed partnerships with computer game companies Eidos (perhaps best known as the developers of the original Lara Croft game), and Rage. This partnership is hard at work developing feature rich games to be delivered through GPRS and 3G – campaigns that make use of games will need to start looking carefully at how and whether they should start making them available on such platforms.

Telecoms providers paid billions of pounds in some countries to win licenses to deliver 3G services. However, the sheer scale of the cost has led many to suggest that the providers won't have the cash to hand to roll out the technology particularly swiftly. The mass market in mobile phones has been very much fuelled by handset subsidies (which are theoretically recouped through the ongoing financial relationship with the customer). The subsidy required to reduce the cost of sophisticated 3G handsets to a level at which they will become attractive to the mass market may just be too much. Indeed, in some countries licences have even been handed back by providers who feel development would not be financially viable. It may be some time before campaigns need to be conducted on 3G.

JD Power's mobile phone survey showed the proportion of people interested in using mobile devices to access the net had fallen from 33 per cent in January 2000 to just 15 per cent in 2001. Similarly, a study by consultancy AT Kearney and the Judd Institute of Management at Cambridge University has shown that interest in using m-commerce (transactions by mobile device) has fallen year on year from 29 per cent to 14 per cent across Europe.

One medium that may be under-utilised at present is PDA devices (such as Palm Pilots). Once again, although the number of PDA users who connect their devices to the net may still be relatively small it includes a large number of journalists who rather like the ability to 'hotsync' (download from their PC) all the latest speeches and press releases and read them on the go. The number of public users is likely to increase rapidly and there will also be a blurring between PDAs and mobile phones creating a need for similar content formats.

Old fashioned text messaging may prove to be the most powerful wireless tool for campaigners due to its sheer popularity. If one bought a mobile phone in 1995 it would be SMS enabled, but who would you be able to send messages to apart from yourself?

However, almost all phones sold in Europe are now digital handsets and, as a consequence, text message capable. About 75 per cent of European phone owners make use of the feature (compared to just 27 percent in the United States). In the UK, text message volumes have increased threefold in the past year according to the GSM Association. Twelve billion messages are expected to be sent in 2001. Five years ago, phone owners sent 0.4 messages a month on average, now they send 35. World volumes are predicted to be over 25 billion a month by the end of 2001 and 200 billion a month by the end of 2002.

Such growth in text messaging has been chiefly among the young. According to JD Power, 90 per cent of new phone handsets sold in the UK in the last quarter of 2000 were pre-paid phones with the market driven by teenage users – chiefly 16 and 17 year olds.

A user study of over a thousand 16 to 30 year olds by the Mobile Channel in early 2001 found that 94 per cent were happy to receive text message advertising if they also received some form of phone cost subsidy as a consequence. The same study found 10 to 20 per cent response rates to such adverts – though apparently giveaways and deals featured heavily in the messages. It will be interesting to see how a medium that has grown to become so popular as a result of friends sending each other messages will be shaped by an onslaught of commercial use.

The latest Big Brother series sold pre-paid cards in newsagents that allowed users to sign up for regular text message updates. Thousands did so in what was perhaps the biggest test of the premium paid-for text message market yet. The market for the receipt of paid-for text messages is expected to grow to £850 million within 12 months.

During the General Election campaign the Labour Party sent tens of thousands of text messages to supporters who had subscribed to the service via the Party's website. These included a message sent shortly before last orders on a Friday night promoting Party policy on licensing reform. Visitors to the Party site were also able to send one of ten campaign messages to friends and colleagues – this proved a highly popular campaign tool and attracted significant press and broadcast coverage. The combination of a mobile phone number and postcode is a powerful one that can be used to narrowcast time and geographically sensitive information such as ministerial visits.

4.3 • The new internet

➥ Call charges are starting to become a thing of the past. Over a quarter of dial-up surfers are now using un-metered providers, paying a monthly fee and using a freephone number to dial in.

Un-metered and high bandwidth solutions such as ADSL and cable modems are gaining a foothold in the residential market (over a third of users are already using some form of un-metered access according to an Oftel survey published in July). BT has recently cut the wholesale price of its ADSL solutions and cable providers, Telewest and NTL, have joined forces to promote their cable modem solutions. These moves will result in a larger proportion of the population being in a position to take full advantage of bandwidth intensive video applications and campaigns. Campaigns in the future may have to consider how to make best use of the broadband environment.

A rapidly growing number of people in the UK now access the web through their digital television set. Of the the major Interactive Digital TV (iDTV) service providers, only ITVDigital say that they give access to the full web, rather than building a 'walled garden' of a few hundred key sites.

National party websites may have the clout to negotiate their way into the 'walled gardens', but the reality for smaller parties and local party websites may be rather different.

At the same time as the number of channels for content delivery is expanding rapidly, there is an increasing blur between many of them. See for example sites such as www.liverpoolfc.tv which are gearing up to deliver paid for match coverage through a web-based medium. As the web and TV merge and become more similar, of what relevance is the prohibition of political advertising on television when a party can spend, spend, spend online? This prohibition has become something of a sacred cow in recent years and it has been argued that British politics will degenerate into a poor imitation of the US system. But the malaise in US politics isn't just down to TV advertising. Rules designed decades ago are surely of little relevance in the information age.

Politics will need to become more visible, as well as relevant and accessible. What better way to increase that visibility than allowing parties to get their message across on TV? The Electoral Commission and the new Ofcomm are certainly going to have to consider what to do about new methods of electronic communication. The fear is that they may cut back on online advertising innovation altogether – a truly retrograde step that should be opposed.

Sites stand or fall by the nature of their content. If a site features compelling news, photos or feature pieces, then surely this should be streamed to other sites operated by local parties, sympathetic organisations and news portals. XML is a language that can be used to format a wide variety of information and facilitate portability. XML and headline exchange streams such as Netscape's RDF should be created by parties and campaigns for integration into other sites.

4.3 • Campaigning in the coming age of the internet election

➡ Electronic and online voting could make polling day (or days) rather different. Traditionally, parties have placed activists on polling stations to collect the polling numbers of those who come to vote. These numbers are then cross referenced to produce a list of supporters who haven't yet voted and whose doors need to be knocked on. If people start to vote online or use their phones will the powers that be wish to provide a live feed of polling numbers to local parties?

New Hal can make his own calls, but in the US, automated telephone systems are frequently used by campaigns to deliver fundraising or GOTV (Get Out the Vote) messages from candidates or key endorsers. It would be interesting to see how the British public, now used to the frustration of calling menu driven call centres, would react to being rung by a machine and played a recorded message. Such systems are relatively cost effective, allowing thousands of calls to be made in a very short space of time with minimal labour costs. If integrated into the campaign's other ICT systems this could become a powerful tool – auto calling of supporters to remind them to vote can take place in minutes with little effort and great effect.

Senator John McCain's campaign to win the 2000 Republican Presidential nomination saw great use made of online canvassing banks. Active supporters could log in to a special section of the website and receive details of people to call and talk to on behalf of the campaign. This hasn't yet been seen in the UK, perhaps because of security and data protection concerns, perhaps because of database integration issues or perhaps just because of suspicion and control freakery. The Frank Dobson for Mayor campaign used a network of volunteers to provide a virtual e-mail call centre that ensured personalised e-mail responses to most incoming mail within 24 hours.

New Hal is able to establish dialogue with a voter through any electronic communication channel. A modern political party needs to be able to do the same – however, unlike Hal, they can't create 'instant' content and policy on the fly. Parties will need to behave in an even more sophisticated way than they like to believe they do at the moment.

Pollsters will be supplemented with 'data mining' experts to crunch the raw statistics generated by new systems. More investment in policy and research teams will be needed to highlight policy areas of relevance to very narrowly targeted groups and to provide them with useful statistics showing the effects of those policies in action. Call centres will need to be able to cope with handling large volumes of electronic messages and provide personal and relevant responses within a matter of hours. The investment in staff, planning and new technology will place even more of a drain on meagre party resources, but could pay dividends in a greatly improved dialogue with the electorate. Perhaps now is the time to once again consider the thorny issue of state funding of political parties.

4.4 • Security and best practice

➡ With the collection, integration and aggregation of so

much information about individuals, it is crucial to maintain a clear, open and transparent privacy policy. A commercial company can get away with sailing close to the wind in its use of information, but the public should be able to expect better of those who aspire to represent them. With a degree of identity checking built in a secure fashion, it should be possible to allow individual electors to view much (or all) of the information that political parties hold about them without having to write a letter and send in a 'nominal' fee.

With the need for privacy also comes the need for security. Although your credit card details are far more likely to be stolen when a waiter whisks your card away from the table than they are in an e-mail, this shouldn't allow a slap-dash attitude. Surfers will expect campaigning sites to use encryption for data in exactly the same way as e-commerce sites do. Security certificates can be purchased from providers such as Thawte for around sixty pounds per year – an investment that will pay itself back many times over in terms of increased donations and fewer sleepless nights worrying about negative press coverage when every one of your donors' credit card numbers is intercepted en route to your server.

In the US, a number of companies provide a third-party service to take online donations for political and other campaigns. The relevant forms can be customised to have the same look and feel as the campaign site, but the transactions actually take place on a different server. Such services are likely to start appearing in the UK with costs recouped from either a service charge or a percentage commission. It may make sense for national parties and campaigns to offer such a service to their local branches – either by negotiating a special deal with an external provider or developing their own bespoke systems.

Nothing could be more embarrassing for a party or campaign than for individuals' private data to be vulnerable to hackers or displayed on a site as a result of a programming glitch. Credit card information volunteered for membership or donations is particularly sensitive. A bad news story about site security will lose the trust of visitors and the volume of online transactions of any description is likely to fall. The encryption basics discussed previously should be supplemented by the separation of web and personal content.

Only that information needed for delivering elements of personalisation should be made accessible through the webserver and these can be coded in such a way as to make this data particularly boring, unhelpful or unintelligible to a hacker.

Access rights to different types of data should be segmented and where credit card or other sensitive information needs to be stored it should be on a system that can only be accessed from a particular location rather than through a publicly available webserver.

But, at the end of the day, so many security breaches are due to passwords being scribbled on Post-It notes or using the name of your cat. Important password data should not be stored on unsecured machines. They should be obscure, changed regularly and only given to people on a 'need-to-know' basis. Passwords for root access to servers or for the editorial control 'god' should be safely locked away.

Web bugs are images or other devices on a web site that cause part of the web page to be retrieved from a completely different web site. When this happens the second web site gets to know that you visited the original web site. The most common web bugs are banner ads. This can bring up potential issues of abuse of information and allows third parties such as ad agencies to determine the IP address of your computer (a unique identification of a computer), the page that you visited, and, more disturbingly, can use cookie information to track your movement across a whole range of sites on which that third party places its 'web bugs'.

Just ten web bug users including ad agency Doubleclick, UK ISP Demon.net, Microsoft's LinkExchange and Yahoo were to be found on seven and a half per cent of sites in a SecuritySpace.com sample of over 200,000 websites. In the US, the Republican Party found itself in hot water when accused of using such 'web bug' techniques to track the movements of voters across the net.

4.5 • Creating the right infrastructure

➡ The decision about the type of software infrastructure one uses in the e-campaign architecture is an important one. Generally, one has two choices: open (generally free or low cost) or closed source (usually attracting a licence fee) software. With open source software, programmers are able to view the source code for a piece of software, modify and redistribute it. The original software itself has no cost attached to it, but the programmer is able to charge for their time and expertise in modifying, configuring or customising that software to meet the particular needs of a project.

There are cost advantages imbued in not having to pay for a licence for proprietary software such as operating system or database technology. If your organisation is fortuitous enough to have volunteer programmers then you may be able to get away with paying almost nothing at all.

There are other potential advantages too. The collaborative nature of the open source movement means that there are a large number of people who will improve and adapt the software, fixing any bugs swiftly and efficiently. Many developers of applications based on underlying Open Source software will then release those applications under the very same terms.

This rapid development, using a large base of highly skilled programmers, can lead to advantages in the speed, stability and security of the software itself.

This is perhaps the key reason for the rapidly growing popularity of systems such as Linux, Apache and PHP. Software is rigorously tested by a large base of users and is designed to do a particular job efficiently rather than suffer from the cumbersome 'feature bloat' found in many commercially developed packages.

The emphasis is also very much on the creative use of the software and using building blocks to create a system that more accurately meets the needs of an organisation than a proprietary one size fits all solution.

Netcraft.co.uk undertake regular surveys of the webservers used on the net. Their July 2001 survey encompassed over 32 million sites and showed Apache, an open source system, held almost 60 per cent of the market, well over twice as much as the second placed Microsoft Internet Information Server (of which we heard so much during the Code Red virus scare).

PHP is a scripting language used to provide interactivity and functionality within a web page, hopefully making it rather different from just an online brochure. It is Open Source software too and Netcraft's latest survey shows that it is now used on almost seven million domain names, compared to just over one million 18 months ago. In July 2001 almost 1.6 million people viewed over 14 million pages at the home page for the software (source: Webalizer analysis of PHP.net logfiles).

Perhaps the best known piece of Open Source software is the operating system Linux. Developed by Linus Torvalds while at Helsinki University, Linux is based on the Unix operating system. It is robust, freely available and comes in many flavours all with a common 'kernel' over which Torvalds still has the final say. Rapidly establishing itself as the operating system of choice for computers serving content on the web, the White House recently switched their sites to a Linux platform because of security concerns.

The PHP, Apache and Linux combination was used to serve Al Gore's campaign website which proudly trumpeted its Open Source credentials. In contrast George W Bush's site made use of proprietary Microsoft technology. In the UK, the Labour Party used the Open Source trio for collection, targeting and distribution of bulk e-mail and text messages, its interactive maps, mortgage calculators, and WAP/PDA sites.

The Conservative and Liberal Democrat sites both made use of custom written ColdFusion scripts to drive their sites. ColdFusion is another web scripting language similar to PHP and now part of the burgeoning Macromedia empire.

Creating bespoke solutions allows the needs of an organisation to be analysed and met. Focus groups of those who will update and run the site can be combined with a study of internal workflow and working practices to design a system that allows those responsible for getting the message out to forget about the technology and focus on honing the message.

Securityspace.com's study of technology penetration in over 200,000 websites showed that just over 4 per cent of them made use of Flash animation technology (despite the fact that apparently over 90 per cent of browsers are able to view it). None of the UK parties made major use of Flash animations during the election campaign, though some used the same technology to produce games and screensavers. Flash is a very 'visual' tool and Flash driven sites are often very poor at providing easily navigable text based content. The technology is however very well suited to producing animated banner adverts and it is surprising that more of these weren't seen in the 2001 UK election.

Just under 8 per cent of web sites make use of cookies to store information about users and track repeat visitors to sites.

Cookies are vital to providing a highly personalised user experience and this low usage demonstrates the relatively unsophisticated nature of much of the net. Most large commercial sites do make use of cookies in increasingly sophisticated ways and we are likely to see this mirrored within political parties – not just for personalisation, but also to allow quite complex data mining about user habits.

Mick Morgan, formerly of the CCTA Government computer agency was quoted in e-Government Bulletin as saying 'The defence research agency DERA and the intelligence community use open source a lot, particularly for network penetration testing since most of the tools used for this are open source.'

Apparently the spooks love the reassurance of being able to have access to the original source code and be certain it contains no bugs or security flaws.

The growth of the Open Source movement as well as the ready availability of simple to use page layout packages, free hosting and online site-building tools, has allowed the growth of real grassroots internet activity. Open Source often provides the wide variety of plug-ins for many low budget sites to make them database driven, collect e-mail addresses, send e-postcards, deliver content to mobile devices and many other features.

Along with robust and easy to use software platforms, a campaign needs to have hardware to deliver high levels of availability and low download times. Increased use of video streaming and MMS will require the use of service providers with high levels of spare bandwidth available on demand. Multiple servers that take up the strain if one fails and regular backups are necessary. The Labour Party experienced such high levels of use of its site (several hundred requests a second were made for the manifesto on the day of its launch) that they engaged the services of a company that specialises in internet load balancing to distribute the content over hundreds of servers. Surfers using anything more than a normal modem saw the site's pages appear almost instantly.

Most local, regional and national interest groups, parties and campaigns have at least one or two enthusiastic internet amateurs who are able to quickly establish an online presence that allows them to organise their supporters and disseminate their message to an interested audience. Local newspapers will give coverage to a local campaign purely because it has some activity on the web.

Many of these online campaigns may be poorly designed, with garish graphics and hard to use navigation. However, some of the more innovative ones almost seem as if they were put together by a professional online campaign consultant. Tips on everything from programming to voter relationship management, privacy and security policies can be found online and quickly adapted to meet the needs of diverse groups.

Everything from vote swapping initiatives and discussion sites for floating voters to local traffic calming campaigns can now find its net niche. This is the truly empowering nature of the internet. Political parties should recognise, accept and engage with this new culture of online activism, but in no way is it their job to try and do it themselves.

Political parties have already started to take some of these lessons onboard. The 2001 election may not have been the internet election, but there was a certainly a greater investment and understanding of the importance of new communication technologies than ever before.

New Hal may not be that far off after all, and perhaps we have just had one of his 'learning' elections.

5.

The new political machine
Chris Casey

computer [n] A device that computes, especially a programmable electronic machine that performs high-speed mathematical or logical operations or that assembles, stores, correlates, or otherwise processes information.

➥ The arrival of the year 2000 was supposed to be catastrophic for computers around the world. Some space-saving computer code, written long ago by programmers who had no reason to expect it would ever be a problem, was going to wreak havoc on computers everywhere at the stroke of midnight. Or so we had all been told. The fearfully anticipated New Year's Day finally arrived, and happily very few of the ominous predictions actually came to pass. Whether it was the result of heroic worldwide programming efforts to fix the bug, or if the problem had simply been overstated from the start, in the face of all of it's daunting hype, the Y2K bug was decidedly a dud.

political machine [n] a group that controls the activities of a political party

'Political Machine' is a term that carries negative connotations of a democracy derailed by ward bosses, voter fraud and stolen elections. Tammany Hall, a 'political club' in New York City, became synonymous with the term 'political machine' in the 1860s, when under the leadership of William 'Boss' Tweed, it controlled the local Democratic Party, and the votes of many who sought Tammany's favours in the form of jobs, city services, and public contracts. Most Americans would like to believe that political machines in this sense are part of our distant past.

But the usage of words sometimes evolves over time, with new meanings applied to fit changing circumstances. Can the internet bring new meaning to the term 'political machine'?

JCR Licklider was the first Director of the Information Processing Techniques Office at ARPA (the US Department of Defense agency directly responsible for the creation of the network technology and protocols we know today as the Internet). He foresaw the political uses of the machine he helped to build to meet military needs. Licklider imagined what he called 'home compute consoles' and television sets linked together in a massive network. 'The political process,' he wrote, 'would essentially be a giant teleconference, and a campaign would be a months-long series of communications among candidates, propagandists, commentators, political action groups, and voters. The key is the self-motivating exhilaration that accompanies truly effective interaction with information through a good console and a good network to a good computer.' Licklider nailed it perfectly, describing the required elements of the new political machine his agency would eventually develop; information, a network, computers, and self-motivated individuals.

Interestingly, it is the mechanical components of the new political machine that are best understood, and least worthy of lengthy discussion. The 'consoles' that Licklider described are the personal computers that can be found in about half of American homes in the year 2000. In fast growing numbers, the owners of these personal computers are connecting them to the 'network' that Licklider helped to build – the internet. From dial-in modems, via cable, and through wireless connections, the number of ways to connect to the network (from an increasing variety of devices) continues to grow and improve.

The component of the machine that deserves the closest examination is the information, and the individuals who seek it. An informed citizenry is generally considered to be an essential component of any working democracy. America's third president, Thomas Jefferson, author of America's founding document *The Declaration of Independence*, wrote;

If a Nation expects to be ignorant and free in a state of civilization, it expects what never was and never will be ... if we are to guard against ignorance and remain free, it is the responsibility of every American to be informed.

Who are these individuals upon whose shoulders that fate of Democracy rests? The easy answer is 'everybody'. As new technology gradually gains widespread acceptance by a significant majority of the population, observers can view the transition as if it were a horse race, speculating on which segment of the population is currently using the technology, and which will be first to cross the line. But eventually all horses will cross the line, and everyone will be online. This is not to suggest we'll ever see perfect saturation, 100 per cent of America's population, or 100 per cent of the world's population for that matter, all surfing the web and merrily sending instant messages to each other. But, for argument's sake, an effective saturation of usage by a significant majority of the populace will serve this understanding of 'everybody'. Who has access to fire, to electricity, to radio, to phone service? In effect, everybody. So it will be with the net.

But let's not settle for the easy answer. To say that 'eventually everybody' will be online is just too easy, and perhaps not very convincing for potential information providers whose time and efforts are required today. According to the US Census Bureau, the U.S. Population is 284,785,202 (US Population Clock, United States Census Bureau, 30 July, 2001). Surveys on internet usage in America show that the number of American adults with internet access grew from about 88 million to more than 104 million in the second half of 2000 (The Pew Internet & American Life Project, February 2001). Worldwide there are 429 million people with access to the Internet (Nielsen/NetRatings stats as reported by *The Register*). On the demographic breakdown of the American online population, the report stated, the increase in online access by all kinds of Americans highlights the fact that the internet population looks more and more like the overall population of the United States.'

And what were these millions of self-motivated individuals doing online? In addition to sending and receiving e-mail, they were finding information of many different types. Seeking out hobby-related information, shopping, medical information, work-related research, financial information, browsing for fun, and general news are among the most frequently reported online activities reported in the Pew survey.

Information is the final and most important component of this machine. It is the petrol without which the engine won't run. And if it should ever run out, the machine will grind to a screeching halt. Fortunately, we have information in great abundance, from a startling variety of sources, with which to fuel this machine. Invention requires imagination. Improvement relies on invention. Did Alexandar Graham Bell imagine the cell phone? Or the Wright brothers imagine the Space Shuttle? Perhaps, but these improvements to their inventions fell to their successors. The many types, sources and uses of the information that feeds the political machine, will shape its development from the current early model, through future advances and improvements that we can only try to imagine today. Another post-election survey found that 'convenience' was found to be the most often stated reason for seeking election news and information online (The Pew Internet & American Life Project, 3 December, 2000). In most cases, netizens turned to the online offerings of well known news organizations including those run by broadcast organizations (cnn.com, msn.com), print publications (washingtonpost.com, nytimes.com), and other news portals (Yahoo, AOL).

Are netizens doing more than just finding information? Are they finding new ways to participate? The Pew report concluded that many who sought political information online, particularly younger voters, found this information to be influential in deciding on how to cast their vote. And this, of course, is a point of no small significance. But the promise of the new political machine lies in motivating individuals to do more than just inform themselves. They need to be convinced to take some action (online or off), and this is where there is the most room for improvement on the current machine. The Pew survey found that a minority of online users made the move from newsgathering to online action.

> The online audience for election news has shown less interest in engaging in other political activities than it has in accessing political information. But the Internet is beginning to affect the way candidates and voters interact. A sizable minority of those who went online for election news (35 per cent) registered their views in internet political polls, while 22 per cent used email to contact candidates and 5 per cent made campaign contributions over the Internet.

Candidates should not be discouraged that news organisations are the primary destination for individuals who are seeking political information online. They should be thankful. Hypertext, or more simply links, are the nature of the web. So it should be no surprise that yahoo.com and nytimes.com were among the top referrers delivering traffic to Hillary Clinton's

New York Senate campaign web site. And that's what the web does, it allows self-motivated and interested individuals to dig as deep into a subject as their time and interest desire. As other candidates likewise did online, then aspiring Senator Clinton used her web site to distribute information about her candidacy, to develop an electronic mailing list of supporters, to recruit volunteers willing to share their time and talents with her campaign, and to accept online contributions.

As political campaigns and parties seek to benefit from the new political machine, and to develop their own use of the net, they would do well to study the still brief history of what's happened so far. Since 1992, much useful experience has been gained, and many valuable lessons learnt by campaigns that have ventured online. Still more experience is gained year after year in conducting online political campaigns in countries around the world. Each election enlarges the class of experienced net campaigners. As experience is gained and shared, improvements and innovations follow. The development of the new political machine is an open source project. While still a very new campaign tool, some fundamentals for using the new political machine are becoming clear. Among them are integration, an early start, and the power of e-mail.

Any candidate that wants to go online should look first. They may be surprised to find that they're already there. Sound silly? Yes, but for too many campaigns, the use of the internet is so peripheral that the candidate and their senior staff seem unaware of their own online efforts. What they find is likely to be an off-message effort by a forgotten campaign staffer or an eager volunteer. The most successful net campaigns are those that are most integral to the overall campaign. At the simplest level, this must mean that the candidate and senior staff must have a working familiarity with the content and functionality of their own web site. A more appealing ideal is a campaign in which an internet strategist is a core member of the campaign team, working with other key campaign personnel such as the campaign manager, press secretary, and media consultant, to integrate the e-campaign into the overall campaign strategy.

As a tool for politics, the new political machine should not be used in isolation from more traditional campaign tools, but in conjunction with them. Most obvious is the use of traditional campaign tools for site promotion. All campaign materials should include the web address, letterhead and business cards, flyers and handouts, direct mail pieces and TV commercials. Do not just rely on supporters stumbling across your site; help them to find you. The ideal here is a candidate who frequently mentions their URL, and who doesn't miss an opportunity to promote it on podiums and in the speeches they give while standing behind them. Likewise, the web site needs to track the rest of the campaign. It needs to look like the rest of the campaign, and to be current with news and information from the campaign.

Successful e-campaigns will launch early. The longer your campaign is online, the greater amount of time available during which voters might visit, volunteer, or perhaps even make a contribution to the campaign. New York Senate candidate, Hillary Clinton, launched a web-site for her 'campaign exploratory committee' on the same day she announced it in the first week of July, 1999, a full 15 months before Election Day. Even if it will be months before the campaign is in full swing, being online early provides candidates an opportunity to stake their online claim and begin some of the groundwork that will pay off later as the campaign becomes more active. Such an early site need not be an all singing, all dancing web site. In fact, a simple placeholder site with some basic functionality is all that is needed to get started. An early launch site can be little more than a logo branded welcome message and an opportunity to subscribe to a mailing list for subsequent updates. And if the opportunity to contribute is made available even at this early stage, so much the better.

Work the web by using e-mail. While web sites garner the majority of the attention for any candidate's online campaign, the electronic mailing lists that are generated by the sites can prove to be an even more powerful tool for communicating with and activating supporters. The Bush and Gore campaigns sent e-mail updates with increasing frequency in the final days prior to election day, to hundreds of thousands of voters (*USA Today*, 3 November 2000). Congressional candidates likewise collected e-mail addresses from supporters and others interested enough to join their mailing lists, inviting the campaign into their in-boxes to provide campaign updates. This is a power of online campaigning that should not be underestimated. Even dedicated campaign supporters may not find the time to visit their candidate's web site with the same frequency that you can expect net users to check their e-mail. Any candidate should utilise their electronic mailing lists to stay in touch with their supporters, keep them 'in the loop' with news of the campaign, and encourage their continued support. Staying in touch with supporters via e-mail works. Hillary Clinton's Senate campaign sent out about fifty such e-mail updates between August 1999 and election day in November 2000. In the period immediately following the sending of an e-mail update, her web site would see a spike in traffic, an increase in the number of online contributions, and new subscribers joining the mailing list.

Along with the opportunity to reach out to their mailing list subscribers, candidates must also accept the responsibility that comes with using e-mail. It is essential that campaign web sites have a clearly stated privacy policy which describes exactly how any personal information collected via the campaign's web site may be used. And it is equally important that subscribers to a mailing list have the means to remove themselves from that list, something they might be expected to do if a campaign abuses the privilege by overwhelming them with too much e-mail.

Many campaigns have utilised electronic post cards as a means for allowing supporters to help spread the word of the campaign to their own friends and family. This can be effective in a number of ways; first in that the messages will arrive from a familiar sender and not appear as an unsolicited message from the campaign, and second, because the recipient usually needs to follow a link and visit the site in order to retrieve their campaign postcard. Pennsylvania Senate candidate Rick Santorum was one of the many campaign web sites that provided such a post card feature. Al Gore's campaign site employed a new twist on this feature by allowing visitors to his campaign site to send their friends a personalised message that contained a return link to any page on his site. This allows people to do their own content targeting, sending information from the site that they think their friends may find of particular interest, rather than just selecting from an existing collection of post card templates. With increased use of HTML formatted or graphical e-mail, it's easy to foresee even more elaborate use of e-mail by campaigns to come. Presidential candidate Steve Forbes utilised streaming media technology from RadicalMail to embed audio and video messages into graphical e-mail messages sent to supporters.

Innovations can often come more quickly online than off. But it is important to keep in mind that the new political machine as imagined more than 40 years ago by JCR Licklider is still an early prototype. In a very short amount of time, the online efforts undertaken by campaigns in the ten year span of 1991 – 2001, will be seen as the simple, yet fundamental efforts in the development of this machine. They are akin to Alexander Graham Bell's call to Watson over a short piece of wire, or the Wright Brothers' flight over a distance they'd have more easily walked. They are the foundation for innovations to come.

Has the internet failed to live up to its hype in the world of politics? Or has the hype simply outpaced reality to such an extent that real progress still seems disappointing? Much like the over-hyped expectations for the Y2K bug, unrealistic expectations for the internet to make a powerful political debut through some notable and undeniable impact on campaigning have been doomed to disappoint.

The reality is that the internet's impact will be demonstrated gradually. It will come in steps, and the development of the new political machine will reveal itself more in the advancements made in its use, and through experience gained by those who are figuring it out, and improving it, as they go.

Sources

- The Pew Internet & American Life Project, 'Internet Election News Audience Seeks Convenience, Familiar Names', <>, 3 December, 2000.
- Rainie, L & Packel, D, 'More online, doing more', The Pew Internet & American Life Project'<http://www.pewinternet.org/>, 18 February 2001.
- Richardson, T, '429 million people use the net', *The Register*, <http://www.theregister.co.uk/content/6/19645.html>,12 June 2001.
- United States Census Bureau, 'U.S. Population Clock' <http://www.census.gov>, as of 8:09 PM, EDT, on 30 July 2001.
- USA Today, 'Campaigns Use E-Mail to Get Out Vote' <http://www.usatoday.com/life/cyber/tech/cti761.htm>, 3 November 2000.

6.

Labour: the e-campaign is born
Kate McCarthy and Andrew Saxton

➥ In all the discussion, reports and debates since Labour's general election victory, the role of the internet has been little heard.

The 2001 election was the first general election in which the internet was used as an important integrated campaigning tool by Labour. The challenge for the Party was to use the technology imaginatively, to exploit its strengths – intimacy, depth, speed, interactivity and fun – and to communicate its message. Labour also wanted to establish the internet as an efficient, cost-effective tool that will become increasingly important as more people are online, the technology improves and the internet generation grows up.

When devising Labour's online campaign strategy, the Party identified the audiences that were particularly important to it and built their communication requirements into its plan.

Labour aimed to:

- meet the needs of its audiences by being responsive, fast, accurate, and interactive
- mobilise and support members and activists by providing a depth of resources and a link between head office and the grassroots
- reach out to new audiences, particularly young people, by being non-preachy
- establish Labour's website as a first point of call for journalists and opinion formers
- generate offline news stories that would communicate Labour's message

The e-campaign used a variety of tools to implement the strategy. At the heart of the operation was the website www.labour.org.uk, created as a welcoming, constantly up-to-date, interactive window into Labour's campaign. The site supported Labour eNews, the core of the e-mail strategy, which delivered our message – both political and organisational – to the inboxes of subscribers. Labour also used a number of smaller, targeted websites to engage different audiences and exploit mobile phone technology in pushing our message.

The aim was to be positive, have fun, and to treat the user – a voter and potential supporter – as someone who wanted to make an informed choice. To raise public awareness, the Labour Party URL was made visible at every branding opportunity from literature to billboards, and from party election broadcasts to the lectern from which senior ministers made televised speeches at key moments during the campaign.

During the four-week campaign we estimate that the website ranked within the top 20 most visited sites in the UK with hundreds of thousands of users each spending an average of around nine minutes on the site. Tens of thousands of people downloaded our manifesto and we sent Labour eNews to up to 35,000 supporters a day, connecting the Party across the country and involving those who might not normally receive our message. The internet has become as important a recruitment and fundraising tool as the incoming phone call. During the campaign, innovative aspects of our online campaign led to news stories across old and new media, generating a subsequent increase in traffic to the site.

6.1 • The Website • < http://www.labour.org.uk>

➥ The website was in itself a massive resource of use to Labour activists, journalists and the public alike. At the outset we made one thing clear to our technical people: the needs of the campaign had to drive our use of technology and not the other way round.

One of the most popular and useful features on the website was the interactive map of the United Kingdom. Working closely with Labour's policy unit we were able to publish what has been described as the most comprehensive set of localised campaigning data ever used in a British election. The 'clickable' map displayed, quickly and easily, tangible policy delivery facts and figures for every constituency on major policy areas including the NHS, school standards, pensions, mortgages, child benefit and crime. Local activists in particular found this focus on delivery an invaluable resource when creating leaflets and newsletters, canvassing voters and creating local media interest.

The map also provided details of the 1997 result, enabling voters to see what position the parties were in and providing contact details for the Labour candidate. During the election we had around 50 people a day pledging their support for Labour via the actions page linked to the interactive map. Each of these was followed up by e-mail or telephone, putting them in touch with their local campaign.

In the final ten days of the campaign we published a two-page campaign diary, one page with pictures and copy from local campaigns around the country (which activists sent in electronically) and the other with an exclusive diary featuring pictures from Deputy Prime Minister John Prescott's battlebus. This was a successful attempt at giving the site a sense of freshness, drawing people in by making it friendlier and more intimate as polling day approached.

There was much discussion of the usefulness and desirability of chatrooms or bulletin boards for the site. Because we judged that most of those who were likely to spend time in an internet chatroom on our site would have already decided which way to vote, we decided against one for the public area of the site. We wanted our supporters to use their time convincing undecided voters and also didn't want to waste our time with people who would definitely be voting against the Party. We did, however, build a bulletin board on one of two password-protected areas of the site, for Labour councillors to exchange views and tactics. The other password-protected area was for party members. Each of these areas was accessed by a self-created password and became a resource and information centre for the relevant group, allowing access to, for example, leaflet templates and logos for literature.

We wanted to establish with journalists early on that the site could be a reliable and useful resource during the campaign. Reporters would often use the website as a first point of call before contacting our press office, taking pressure off staff there. Journalists could download documents and manifestos from the site, read speeches as they were being delivered, get press releases immediately, and download pictures and audio and video clips.

For the first time in a general election, every press conference from Millbank Tower, and some from around the country, was webcast live and archived on the site for 24 hours. The Labour site also featured live webcasts of other events, for example question and answer sessions with the Prime Minister, using new mobile webcasting technology, developed especially for Labour and used for the first time during the election. Webcasting fitted in perfectly with Labour's principles of openness and accountability

Statistics from an earlier incarnation of the site suggested that our policy pages were among the most popular features. So in the run-up to the campaign, the Party increased the amount of information available – there were over 80 areas of policy detailed on the site, enabling users to find a depth and breadth of information on the topic of interest to them, even if it wasn't making headline news. There is no other way to easily provide voters with detailed policy positions on such a range of issues. We prided ourselves on the fact that (unlike the other parties) we had such a richness of policy information, but also that we linked each policy area to speeches, press releases, questions and related policy areas, so the reader could always find out more. By the end of the campaign the site had grown enormously and contained nearly 1,000 pages.

6.2 • E-mail

➥ Labour's e-mail strategy was based on the same principles as the website. The Party needed its messages to be open and accessible and written in such a way that readers felt positive towards Labour. We didn't want to launch into attacks on our opponents.

We set up a permission-based system whereby people gave us their e-mail addresses and some basic information about themselves which allowed us to target the information we were sending. During the four-week election period we sent over 2.5 million e-mails – at very little cost

Labour eNews was used to link the central campaign strategy and message to activity in the constituencies. Activists copied its content to local constituency members and some subscribers even took on the responsibility of printing out the regular bulletins to share with activists who were not online.

Labour took data protection issues and spamming (the sending of unsolicited e-mails) very seriously from day one. The Party turned down the opportunity of using a number of lists of e-mail addresses (despite these lists containing people we thought would probably be supportive) because we had not been given expressed permission to contact them. We felt it was essential that we respected our audience in this way.

The purpose of eNews was to send Labour's message to its supporters and activists, to build the links between the centre and activists in the field and to encourage people to join, donate, shop and volunteer. It was used extensively in the final days of the campaign to send targeted messages to people in key constituencies highlighting the local reasons to vote for their Labour candidate.

We tried to keep eNews bulletins as concise as possible, with pithy stories – usually about four or five per bulletin, with links back to the site. The content was always balanced between policy and organisation, local and national, and reflected the themes of the day, e.g. the manifesto launch and a pensions day. On election day itself eNews took the form of a personal message from Tony Blair.

E-mail was also used to distribute more widely some of the interactive and fun elements of the e-campaign, such as our Cut 'n' Run game – a game highlighting the Tories' £20 billion public spending cuts guarantee.

We wanted also to offer users the chance to tailor eNews to their requirements. People could choose from eight policy areas, request daily or weekly bulletins and supply us with their mobile phone number if they wanted to receive text messages

6.3 • Spin-off sites

➥ However large and comprehensive the main Labour site was, it wasn't able to meet all our aims, so we developed a host of micro sites aimed at particular user groups and purposes.

At the beginning of the campaign Labour launched www.ruup4it.org.uk with the aim of engaging young people in the democratic process. This site featured a non-Labour branded design written in a way research suggested young people wanted i.e. non-preachy, non-dictatorial and providing a reasonable overview of the political parties and the main political issues.

There was much speculation as to the voting intentions of young people. Research suggested that first-time voters were reluctant to vote or were turned off by politics. It also highlighted that young voters tended to favour Labour and had made it clear that they wanted political information via the internet. Tens of thousands of people visited the site and our feedback indicated that the site at least offered an inroad to addressing an audience that was said to be disengaged with politics.

A 'compare and contrast' page asked people to agree or disagree with certain statements in order to find out where they stood on the political barometer, a political history page gave perspective and depth and we also linked to other online political resources, including the Tory and Liberal Democrat sites.

Other pages featured endorsements from first-time voters and celebrities, games and a text message competition where people could win prizes by voting for their favourite text message. Fifty thousand scratch cards and a similar number of flyers were distributed by Labour student groups and drove interest in the site. It received good coverage in national newspapers and radio.

Labour did not expect to change the course of the election with this site, but felt the need to have a go at doing something that might help increase interest and boost turnout among 18-24s. The Party could not sit back and do nothing and, as the Hansard Society noted in its report of the election and the internet, in terms of energising the youth vote, ruup4it.org.uk was 'far more than any other party attempted.'

Our hunch was that first-time voters would also be among the first to embrace and continue to use new technology – a MORI poll found that 81 per cent of 15-24-year-olds use text messaging on their mobile phones every day. Another found that 24 per cent of 18-24s would look online for news and information about party politics and nearly a quarter of first-time voters said they would use the internet to help them decide how to vote (*Guardian*, 2001). With 82 per cent of 16-24s having internet access, using the net to reach young voters has to be firmly built into the campaign next time. It will be too risky not to do it. In the 1950s some observers thought television would be a nine-day wonder. Young people will continue with these technologies and will be open to new ideas like WAP and

PDA and other new technologies, and Labour, as a progressive Party, must make use of these opportunities.

- http://www.toriesslashpublicservices.com A one-page site with an audio message from a William Hague impersonator admitting the Tories were 'in a bit of a pickle' after their plans for cutting public services by £20bn. We drove traffic to the site by distributing e-mails with a teaser message linking to it.
- http://whyeducationmatters.com was mentioned in our mini manifesto and linked to a special page on the main site.
- http://www.youdecide.org.uk An interactive comparison site with a list of statements with which users could agree or disagree, press a button and find the Labour and Tory position on those statements. Links went back to the policy section of the main site.

6.4 • Text messaging

➡ During the last week of the campaign we offered what we believe was a first for a British political party. Website visitors were able to send get-out-the-vote messages to their friends and colleagues via our site, resulting in tens of thousands of messages urging people to vote Labour on election day. This provided a valuable media hit and was fun for senders and receivers alike. Our text message about reforming the licensing laws – which arrived on people's mobiles in the hour before pub closing time on the Friday before the election, generated front page news.

We also sent out five bulk text messages during the last week of the campaign. Our messaging was, like eNews, carefully controlled to avoid spamming. On election day itself we sent two messages aimed at getting out the vote. On Saturday 9 June we sent a thank you message.

6.5 • Off the shelf websites for Labour Party representatives

➡ After numerous inquiries we took the decision to offer a purpose-built website service, Web-in-a-box, produced by an outside agency and for which users needed very little web knowledge to edit. Around 85 MPs, Constituency Labour Parties, MEPs, Scottish MSPs, Welsh AMs and Councillors signed up for the service which included a central updating service of headline news as well as links to the main party site.

6.6 • Conclusion

➡ Labour wanted to ensure that its first true e-campaign went smoothly and surely, laying the groundwork for the internet to play a significant and integrated role in the future. We wanted the e-campaign to contribute to the main aims of the Party – to win votes, recruit members, supporters and volunteers, and to raise money.

For the e-campaigns team it was an exercise in demonstrating that here was a medium the Party could use effectively and efficiently to get its message out AND energise members and activists. Once the campaign managers could see what could be done with the web and e-mail we knew they would be keen to use it further, and that is precisely what happened. The web's cost effectiveness and ease of distribution should stand it in good stead.

Getting the site functioning smoothly and built in to the campaign gave us great satisfaction. Strategic decisions at the top level were reflected in the site – every stunt, speech, visit, photo opportunity and announcement had a web angle.

Labour had to build, develop and fine tune the site in a short space of time to ensure that it would meet the challenges and withstand the rigours of a general election, and this it did.

By the time of the next general election campaign, web technology will no doubt have taken another great leap forward and far more people will be online. To match this increase in interest we will be able to include greater personalization of web content and e-mails, offer more interactivity in the way of games, text messages and contact with candidates and improve our e-mail response time. Cheaper and faster internet connections will allow better quality videos and webcasts.

What this election proved for us is that the internet is becoming the bread and butter of political campaigning. It is no longer a case of having the internet as an add-on to the strategy but of making the eCampaign an element in each part of it.

In terms of concrete deliverables as examples of our impact, we could point to the number of online joiners (equal to the number who joined the party via telephone during the election period), the increase in merchandise sales and the high number of clickthroughs from our site to the postal vote and the rolling registration sites.

The number of visitors to the website, the feedback from users and the publicity we generated by being innovative were of great encouragement. The challenge now is to develop our thinking to stay one step ahead of our opponents.

6.6.1 • Acknowledgements

Labour's e-campaign would like to thank staff and party members for embracing the site and the technology, our outside service providers and above all, our trusty band of volunteers, without whom we wouldn't have reached the standards we did.

7.

E-campaigning: active and interactive

Justin Jackson

➥ The internet has already transformed communication. Yet its use by politicians, in the UK at least, lags behind that found in business, media, academia and government. Although there are signs – particularly at the general election of 2001 – that this is changing, there remains much to be done.

I leave it to students of politics to explain why this is the case. This chapter is aimed at campaigners, in the hope that they can build upon the experience of one of their colleagues and avoid their mistakes. My theme is a simple one: the internet can help politicians establish an effective dialogue with the electorate, but they must recognise that it is a distinctive technology that brings with it new possibilities and new challenges.

In short, you need to be one part politico and one part geek.

For the sake of simplicity, I focus on attempts by a party to influence voting behaviour. I begin by looking at what is special about the internet, concluding that its plus points have a longer shelf life than the disadvantages. I then briefly outline a sensible political strategy before seeing how the internet might be harnessed for such a campaign.

It is probably best to get the bad news out of the way. In some respects, the internet suffers in comparison with other channels of communication. Speed remains a problem for most users; while a typical 56k connection is enough to transfer a lot of text, reasonable sized photos and even good quality audio it is still not practical to deliver full motion video without a broadband connection.

Cost is the second issue: as well as an initial investment in equipment, there is also a marginal cost for users who maintain a metered connection. Consequently, not everyone has convenient access to the internet – and the demographic profile of internet users still does not match that of the population at large.

Third, expertise also matters: compared to other ways of communicating – such as the telephone, fax machine or TV – getting online requires a quite astonishing amount of technical confidence, if not skill. Making full use of the internet is, of course, even more demanding. This is an unfortunate obstacle to the internet achieving full penetration and can again skew its demographics.

The fourth hurdle is fidelity: designers can never be sure how their work will appear to the end user. A single website can look very different on a Mac than a PC, under Netscape rather than Explorer or with sixteen colours rather than thousands. Some people may not see anything at all, if a site relies upon a 'plug in' that they have not installed on their machine.

Yet these four drawbacks – low speed, high cost, difficulty of use and low fidelity – are becoming less important. More users are getting broadband access on their fixed connections and will soon enjoy high speed wireless access, too. Metered connections are uncommon and, with the possible exception of a hiccough as we switch to mobile communication, will not return. Confidence in using PCs increases with each generation (whether human or machine) and people increasingly own dedicated devices, which are easier to use. Most commentators expect fidelity, too, to improve as designers write flexible code that can adapt to different platforms and browsers and which coalesces around standards such as W3C.

So, as the bad news turns in to yesterday's news, we shall be left with a channel of communication that has real advantages. They are the focus of this chapter and it is worth spelling them out in full.

First, we can narrowcast across the internet. Communication can be one-to-one, allowing popular services such as e-mail and instant messaging. Even websites, which seem to operate on a one-to-many model, can identify the user (by logging in or using cookies) and tailor their content accordingly. In this, the internet scores an immense advantage over broadcast technologies such as television or radio.

Immediacy is the second characteristic. Although speed is an issue when it comes to transferring large quantities of data, small packets can reach their destination very quickly. Not only does this mean that it is likely to be up-to-date, users can identify themselves and make requests, moments before seeing the effect of these instructions.

Third, the internet is dynamic. As data is transferred between computers, it is easy for those machines to modify the information – or even generate it from scratch – before transmission. This means that outgoing data can react to incoming data, whether part of the ongoing dialogue or received from elsewhere.

It is these three characteristics – narrowcasting, immediacy and dynamism – that allow the internet to be interactive. Traditional communication typically requires human intervention at each stage of the dialogue, yet this is just not so with the internet. Not only can a server respond to explicit requests from a user, it can also react to signals implicit in behaviour. In fact, neither end needs to have a human; machines increasingly interact by themselves, perhaps reporting an error in a piece of software and downloading a patch to fix it.

Channels of communication are, then, affected by the technology. However, this is not the only way in which they are defined: users also acquire expectations, which need to be met. To be sure, some of these expectations ultimately stem from technology: the ease with which information can be gathered across the internet, for instance, has meant that websites feel obliged to provide a privacy policy.

Yet some do not: take the view that unsolicited e-mail ('spam') is more intrusive than traditional junk mail. Accordingly, it is important to check that an individual has given his permission before attempting to engage them in conversation.

The enormous choice that we enjoy on the internet makes it particularly important for participants to understand the rules of the game. Competition is fierce and services that do not meet, or exceed, a user's expectations will soon be discarded. Add to this the need for a user to initiate dialogue, or grant permission for others to do so, and it is easy to see why there are rarely second chances on the internet.

These findings are best applied to political campaigning by seeing how the internet can be deployed as part of a well known (and convincing) strategy, namely that deployed by the Republicans in the US Congressional elections of 2000 and the Conservatives in the British General Election of 2001. As an observer in November 2000 and a participant in June 2001, your author remains convinced that the strategy itself was not at fault in Smith Square. At most, its implementation was less than profound, and other factors played a significant role, too.

The strategy itself is straightforward. People vote for many different reasons. Most of the time, voting is a means to an end: we support a party in order to further certain policies or improve the advocacy of particular interests. When deciding how to vote, we draw upon our knowledge of a party's policies, its competence, its general outlook and loyalties, and its record in government. Of course, most of us have better things to do – getting on with our lives, for one – than worry too much about what the parties are up to. This means that we often vote with partial knowledge and insufficient time carefully to weigh up the alternatives.

A person's concern for her lot and that of her family generate instrumental reasons for voting (let us leave concern for anyone else to one side as, however unrealistic, it does not affect our discussion). She faces problems in her life that need resolution. Some of this is up to her; other problems require, or could benefit from, a change in government policy. She will be looking for a party that, to start with, identifies her concerns – and this means a party that is listening to people like her. Even better is a party that is made up of people like her, dealing with the same issues as she does. Finally, the party has to convince the voter that it has solutions to her problems; it has to persuade her that these solutions are realistic and, moreover, that they are the best people to implement them.

To borrow a phrase from the British Conservatives, but which Republican strategists could just as easily have deployed, a party needs to show that it is listening to people and tackling the issues that really matter to them. To be convincing, it needs to use the language of people, not politicians; it must show that it 'gets it'.

Campaigners rely upon dialogue to provide these instrumental reasons for voting. First, the party must listen to the electorate if it is truly to identify their problems. Second, the party needs to set out how it would improve their lives – outlining its solutions, justifying them and saying how the nation can afford them. Finally, the party must convince the voter that it is trustworthy and competent – highlighting its past record if impressive or, if not, convincing the electorate that it has changed.

The instrumental approach to voting remains quite calculating: what will my vote achieve? Not so for the intrinsic approach: here, voting is an end in itself, regardless of its effect on the election. Our identity might be tied up with support for a political party (canvassers will be familiar with people saying they 'are' Conservative as much as saying they 'vote' Labour) or, more likely these days, with a set of values that we express by supporting a certain party. We should not assume that people refrain from tactical voting because of imperfect knowledge or bounded rationality.

Communication also matters to the intrinsic model. If someone is voting for a party as an expression of their values, then it is clearly just as important to identify these values and show how the party shares them. Dialogue is also critical in reinforcing a relationship that exists with the voter or a community. The fact that the Labour Party is listening to your union is a powerful reason to give it your support.

In what follows, I concentrate upon the role of dialogue in generating instrumental reasons for voting. This does not assume that the voter must recall every conversation that takes place or even commit the relevant ones to memory. That will not happen, of course – if only politicians were that interesting – but an individual's perception of a party is surely coloured by the way it converses with him. If the party uses his language, it understands him. If the party discusses his issues, it represents him. If the party does it effectively, it will deliver. Few campaigners would ask for much more than that.

Unfortunately, life is not that easy. Few channels of communication between a party and the voter are direct. They are mediated by journalists, pressure groups, activists or other voters. This means that a party needs to harness these mediators in its communication strategy, and to do this, it has to understand their motivation. Only then can a party establish an effective dialogue with voters through them. That is why parties hire press secretaries, court the churches and train their activists.

We have seen that the internet is a distinctive channel of communication and explored how dialogue fits in to an effective political campaign. It is now time to bring together these two strands of the discussion. It is easy to see how: the internet is an ideal channel of communication for listening to people and tackling the issues that really matter. Let us consider these in turn.

The parties did not always grasp the importance of listening online. Early efforts failed because they regarded the internet merely as an outgoing channel of communication. Websites were little more than online brochures. E-mail originated from the party and was just another way of spreading the word; incoming messages were lucky to be read, let alone receive a reply. Although the parties now see the error of their ways, sadly this is still not true of many candidates. I have lost count of the number of MPs who refuse to publish an e-mail address for fear of 'too much correspondence' from their constituents.

The voter can never be given too many opportunities to speak out. The party needs to listen – who knows, it may learn something – and to be seen to be listening. At the very least, it needs to publish an e-mail address and ensure that its correspondence unit replies to incoming e-mail at least as fast as traditional letters (faster, preferably, given people's expectations). Yet that is only the beginning. A good rule of thumb is to give the voter the opportunity to respond to anything that the party says or does. This might simply involve the voter expressing a view; but it might include joining the party, volunteering to help or donating cash. That is why we placed a 'Make a Difference' bar on each page of www.conservatives.com, providing opportunities for people to get involved.

Voters expect politicians to listen. It says more about a party than any number of policy launches or press conferences. Yet it is also a valuable source of information both in aggregate, and, more importantly, about the individual elector. This is especially important on the internet because of the unparalleled opportunities for a party to personalise its communication with the voter.

This is our second recommendation. If dialogue is directly relevant to an individual and his family, it demonstrates that the party has been listening. It shows, too, that the party is tackling issues that concern not just the population at large, but subjects that really matter to him and his family. The importance of personalisation – and the extent to which it should be taken – cannot be overestimated. Targeting messages is of little point unless its content is of particular relevance to the recipient – ideally a single recipient. Why address a group when you can speak with an individual?

Personalisation is the most powerful technique available to the parties, but it nevertheless needs to be used with care. Several channels of communication exist between the party and the voter and it is important that they reinforce, rather than cut across, each other. This would be a trivial problem if each channel were personalised, but this clearly does not happen: parties still reach more voters through advertising and the news.

There is a real problem here. Most people have better things to do with their lives than obsess about politics like we do. A party's message will only reach the voter if it adopts a disciplined, laser-like focus. If someone is reading about a party's proposals for a tax cut in her newspaper, watching the announcement on the evening news and driving past posters advertising it on her way to work – what is she to make of the party's website talking about something else entirely, because it has been personalised for her?

I take for granted that all communication with the party is intended to reinforce its core messages (if not, the party might as well call it a day). The question here is different: what is the best way to instil these core messages using successive dialogues? What matters is the likelihood that an individual conversation with the voter will penetrate. If we expect it to score a hit by itself, then put the party's eggs in this one basket and forget about other attempts; if, on the other hand, this engagement with the voter is unlikely to get through on its own, it is best to align its messages with other dialogues. Together, they might have an impact.

This suggests that dialogue should be personalised if it is likely to penetrate by itself (although there is a chicken and egg situation here, in that the more relevant the conversation, the more likely we are to engage the voter – nobody said this would be easy). This depends, in turn, upon three factors.

First, a dialogue is more likely to penetrate if the user initiated it. In these cases, she has demonstrated a clear interest in communicating with the party and, in all likelihood, indicated a desire to talk about a particular topic. Assuming the party's response takes the initial request in to account, it is more likely to score a hit where the user is pulling down information rather than where it is pushing it.

(It is best to understand push and pull as the two ends of a spectrum. E-mail generally hovers around the push pole, such as when we send out a news bulletin; it need not, as when a party sends an email in response to an inquiry from a voter.

Websites, in contrast, are typically found nearer the pull pole; the user needs to visit the site in the first place to initiate the dialogue. Yet huge variation remains: the site might provide the individual with a standard menu from which to choose or, increasingly, provide what it thinks is more relevant upfront.

Second, the significance of any channel fluctuates with the

electoral cycle. A party has a huge advertising budget and receives a great deal of news coverage during a general election. Its online efforts, at the moment at least, cannot compete; they must instead reinforce the broadcast message. In peacetime, the situation is quite different. A party will do away with its advertising budget and find it difficult to interest journalists, especially in opposition. In these circumstances, there are few other channels with which to align communication: the relative likelihood that dialogue across the internet penetrates is greater.

Finally, we need to consider how much trust the individual places in the dialogue. If the channel of communication between party and voter is indirect, then this will largely depend upon the mediator(s). Many people at the last general election, for instance, preferred to get their political news from sites such as Guardian Unlimited or BBC News Online, valuing their analysis and distance from the parties; others wanted to make up their own minds and visited sites run by the parties themselves; some did not actively seek information and formed their impressions based upon contact with candidates and activists.

This means that the party needs to cater both for the voter and these mediators. Ask yourself why a voter visits a party's site or subscribes to its newsletters: they are seeking information about the party and its policies. On www.conservatives.com, voters were provided with copy written for them, rather than journalists; none of the parties would dream of putting press releases through a voter's letter box, so why do they suffice on the internet? The copy was tailored to the medium, too, in that it was short and punchy. Most importantly, it was written 'straight'; if a voter has bothered to visit the party's website, then she is not going to be converted by a political slanging match. They want information in order to make up their own mind.

At the same time, it is important to provide all of the tools that journalists need – press releases, print quality photographs and even audio or video clips. Similarly, activists need to be provided with lines to take, sample letters and other campaigning material. Each audience has different needs. Be aware of them.

Our conclusion is much the same: each channel of communication has distinct characteristics, some good and some bad. Be aware of these too. Campaigning on the internet takes its lead from existing political strategy; the trick is to implement in a way that makes best use of the medium. Parties increasingly have to show that they are listening to the electorate and tackling the issues that matter to them – and the good news is that the internet provides them with a channel of communication well suited to that.

8.

The contagious campaign • (part 2)
Business in the new media era
Anthony Painter

➥ The era of mass media had its tools. The tools employed by business and politics were remarkably similar. If you had an issue of public interest or one that was affected by public policy, you would do one of two things. If it was issue of high technical complexity and of low public salience you would lobby those ministers, officials, councillors or whoever had authority with a well defined case. If the issue was of broader public interest then you would ensure that the right journalists were on your side and hire PR professionals to ensure your message was disseminated and your corporate reputation was protected.

One or both of these methods would usually do the job if your case had any validity at all. It is little wonder that so many people involved in political management ended up working for public relations departments or agencies, or lobbying companies. David Hill, Joy Johnson, and Tim Bell all moved from high-level political roles to the worlds of public relations and lobbying. They were just the senior ones – droves of more minor political professionals migrated into lucrative positions in the private sector. Some were more notorious than others.

The irony of the new media era is that it is actually more difficult and costly to manage the public image of your business. There are three main reasons for this:

1   the public are more savvy and cynical as they have greater access to information and alternative perspectives – they also demand that the products they buy form part of their self-expression and, therefore, companies, like political organisations have to think about personalising their message.
2   campaigning (such as Greenpeace or Friends of the Earth) groups have adapted and adopted new media tools and communication devices in a rapid and often devastating fashion
3   the media through which people have access to images and messages of corporate behaviour are so much more diffuse and unpredictable.

Some businesses have realised that the environment in which they are operating has changed – they've learned from bitter experience. Others vaguely recognise these changes, but to accept the premise that the environment has changed requires a profound challenge to organisational standards and culture as well as communication methods. The old guard will take some time to weaken as there are many vested interests in maintaining the status quo.

It is now necessary to see how changes in the cultural environment that are affecting politics also affect business. Firstly, we will analyse the nature of the changes and their consequences. A mismatch between consumer expectation and corporate delivery will be observed (which, of course, is reminiscent of the political world). Then we will look at two fairly well documented case studies of corporate action. However, one case study is looked at from the perspective of conventional public relations and the other from the perspective of lobbying. Both traditional approaches have failed and they have failed because power is no longer only to be found in Whitehall or in black books filled with journalistic contacts.

8.1 • I have more power but you don't seem to care

➥ The changing environment of corporate communication is both related to the onset of new media and, strangely enough, to the effect of the new environment of politics. Citizens no longer feel empowered by politics but they do feel that consumption is a form of political self-expression. Citizenship has weakened in politics but it has given rise to the 'citizen-consumer' (Scammell, 2000) in the market place. The 'citizen-consumer' expresses the political values they hold in an act of consumption rather than in political participation. Just like the relationship between conventional citizens and political parties, 'citizen-consumers' are motivated, informed and on occasion represented by professional organisations – be they NGOs or lobby groups.

Ninety per cent of respondents in a recent poll expressed a wish for companies to communicate corporate social responsibility (CSR). However, only a third of the public in the same survey were aware of any initiatives (MORI, 2000). There is a striking similarity between this statistic and the fact that people are no less interested in politics than a decade ago but much less likely to participate in any political activity. People are interested but companies are either (a) not conducting themselves in a manner which would win favour with the public or (b) not communicating that fact. Given the positive PR hit to be had out of communicating any CSR initiative, it would seem that companies, in general are just not acting in a way that would reassure the public.

Not only is there an expressed desire for good corporate practice in the social and environmental policies of corporates but there is an increased proclivity for consumers to act on values when making purchases. A survey conducted by MORI for the Co-operative Bank identified five clusters of consumer behaviour when investigating values-based consumer behaviour. It is estimated that 22 per cent of the population 'look after their own' and 49 per cent of the population 'do what they can', which very rarely involves more than buying locally or recycling occasionally.

Five per cent of the population are 'global watchdogs' active in the cause of promoting corporate and environmental responsibility. 18 per cent are 'conscientious consumers' who you won't see manning a street stall on a Saturday afternoon but do place importance on ethical considerations when making purchases. The most intriguing group is the 'brand generation' who make up Six per cent of the population. They are interesting because they make up pretty much the group that we are talking about when looking at voter alienation.

The 'brand generation' is young, middle-class (C1/C2), who don't really like to be called 'ethical' but they do talk a lot about company behaviour. Brand reputation is important for them (MORI, 2000). Their behaviour is exactly what you would expect from this group. Brand is an important part of self-expression and identity and they are willing to go beneath the surface of brand so that it has a more complete meaning. The brand becomes part of a social narrative.

What is clear is that, while a long way from the 'global watchdogs', the 'brand generation' cares about ethical issues, and caring is just one step removed from action. Throughout the population, 55 per cent of people consider themselves to be ethical consumers and, as such, can be considered potential boycotters and discriminators against products which do not achieve their ethical expectations (MORI, 2000).

It is clear why these values are being imported into the market place. Increasingly, both the cultural and economic environments are coming together. Market transactions are invading cultural space and increasingly subsuming it. It is then only logical that values should seep outwards into the market place.

It is in this context of increasing consumer consciousness of the value power of consumption that the modern NGO operates. Of all organisations, a coherent case can be constructed arguing that NGOs have understood the new media environment more than any other type of organisation apart from perhaps the global telecommunications and entertainment giants. They have certainly adapted better to this environment than any other issues based organisation.

In Genoa, Seattle, Stockholm, Berlin, London and Sydney we have seen the devastating effect of this organisation. The trick is not just to spread information (important though that is) but also to latch on to cultural symbols and values. Admittedly, because social and environmental activism is predominantly a young person's activity they have a head start. The subversive nature of the organisations also helps. However, the heady mix of news event management, message dissemination, grassroots organisation, cultural events, and cyber-activism is quite intoxicating.

Before the May Day riots of 2000 and the protests of 2001, it was possible on one web-site, www.urban75.org, to get information on the issues, legal advice if you were going to the protests and the phone number of a sympathetic lawyer if anything went wrong, discussions with fellow participants, news and events and links to other similar organisations. A global site, www.mayday2001.org, gave links to localised information on the protests in 20 different countries. Reclaim the Streets has been successful in unifying political causes with underground music culture for many years (Klein, 2000, 311–323). Greenpeace are past masters at staging protests in order to seize the news agenda – the Brent Spar protests in 1995 immediately spring to mind. The image is always of the little guy against the insensitive global conglomerate – Robin Hood against the Sheriff of Nottingham.

The point is not to advocate that business copies these organisations but that it has something to learn from the mastery of new media devices by these NGOs. It is more challenging for business to get their message across but then this is profits we are talking about and it is definitely worth the investment and effort.

8.2 • When PR goes wrong: the cases of Shell and Esso

➡ Around the mid-1990s Shell was about to hit a nadir in public reaction to its practices. It wasn't to know as it was the first case of a company being fundamentally hit by not understanding the new corporate and cultural environment (incipient as it was) – conventional PR was inadequate and individuals were increasingly transferring their social and environmental values into the market place. The market place is simply becoming an extension of self-expression in an increasingly commoditised cultural realm.

There were two main issues that sparked public reaction to Shell – Brent Spar and the company's presence in Nigeria. Shell was planning to decommission the defunct Brent Spar oil platform and submerge it in the sea. Greenpeace argued that it should be taken back to shore, dismantled, and the materials recycled. Shell, with the backing of the British Government, disagreed. After a Greenpeace demonstration which dominated the news for days, Shell backed down. During the protest period, Shell's sales in Germany declined by at least 20 per cent (Klein, 2000, 380).

Before this incident, Shell had withdrawn from Ogoni Land in Nigeria due to criticisms of the treatment of the Ogoni people.

By the mid-1990s there were two ways for the company to go. Its social and environmental practices were starting to provoke customer reaction and this helped to focus the mind. It could either carry on regardless or it could undertake a fundamental review of its ethical practices and the external cultural environment. It took the second cause of action and has never looked back.

Shell initiated independent reports of its social, environmental and workplace practices. The aim was to create a standard by which it could measure improvement, create transparency for its stakeholders, and imbue its everyday working practices and decision-making with an ethical awareness. Shell set up a web-site www.shell.com/tellshell where individuals could post unmoderated and, therefore, completely honest opinions about Shell's corporate practices. The fact that these discussions were being hosted in Shell's on-line space meant that they could gauge the substance of public concerns and they had a right of reply. The cynical might also say that it also diverted energy from external criticism of Shell practices. Some of the comments on the site are remarkably honest:

'This is the most obvious Greenwash I have yet to see – well done Shell, you've sunk to new levels. It appears your PR agency have successfully managed to convince you that the bulk of the population are morons.'
(Anonymous, People, planet and profits: a summary of The Shell Report)

This comment appeared on both the web-site and in a free summary report concerning Shell's economic, social and environmental report distributed with *National Geographic*. Shell have reviewed their corporate practices, changed behaviour and sought to effectively campaign in the new media environment. The strategy has had considerable success. The company that brought us Brent Spar now seems light-years away. Shell themselves would not argue that there was no room for improvement but they asked the right questions and are now starting to get some reassuring answers.

Contrast this with one of Shell's close competitors, Esso. The Esso case is salutary as here is a company that seems completely unprepared for the new cultural environment in which it finds itself. Adverts for a web-site www.stopesso.com started to appear on the front page of British broadsheet newspapers in summer 2001. The web-site (and the advert) tries to promote the idea of boycotting Esso because its political donations have allegedly contributed to President Bush rejecting the Kyoto Treaty on climate change.

On further investigation, the web-site and publicity campaign surrounding it is the work of a formidable coalition of Greenpeace, Friends of the Earth, and People & Planet. These highly effective campaigning organisations have joined forces to target Esso's bottom-line.

What is Esso's response? Faced with a barrage of negative publicity in the media, negative advertising and campaigning, Esso placed a press release on their UK web-site which runs to 1,000 words of rather defensive self-justification for their actions. It is worth reading just for the explanation of the organisation's political donations – probably entirely factual and genuine, but phrased in such a lawyerly fashion that the reader can't help but doubt what's said. Just as a bonus, you can also download a leaflet on how to save energy at home from the site.

Unlike Shell, which examined the very heart of its business and communications, Esso is trying desperately to paper over the cracks.

It is using the internet, but it has not understood the new media environment. People are increasingly going shopping with their values placed in their purse and unless you can credibly vie for attention in an increasingly fragmentary and momentary media then you might as well not bother. Esso may learn but it is not just short-term profits that should be concerning it now – it is the attitude of an entire generation to its corporate ethics.

8.3 • When lobbying goes wrong: the case of Monsanto

➡ When, as a company, you have an issue that cuts across international regulatory frameworks, becomes an issue of global trade, and is complex in nature, it is traditional to set up a highly professional lobbying operation. The last thing you want in that situation is for the issue to be picked up and forced through the over-simplifications of public debate.

Monsanto's approach to a variety of political issues that it faced, from 'terminator' drugs to intellectually property, was exactly right at first glance. However, these strategies take on a new risk in the modern world. Issues have a habit of finding their way into the public realm through the proliferation of information, consumer awareness and action. If you have been pursuing a strategy aimed at political elites and suddenly you find yourself having to mount a public defence then forget it. It's too late and no matter what you do, the issue is now out of your control.

There is little doubt that Monsanto had some of the strongest advocates that a company could ask for. The Clinton administration had decided that potential European trade action against the growth-hormone rBST could be detrimental for US trade. On the 18 May 1998 he met Tony Blair and had been briefed to warn, 'the EU's slow and non-transparent approval process for genetically modified organisms has cost US exporters hundreds of millions in lost sales (Monbiot, 2001, 242)'. The President of the USA is not a bad advocate to have as advocates go.

Monsanto's lobbying efforts received some success. Genetic labelling was liberalised to a certain extent in Europe and the decision-making process on genetically modified organisms was improved in the favour of Monsanto and other GMO producers. During the 20 months after the 1997 election, Monsanto met with government officials and Ministers on 22 occasions (Monbiot, 2001, 266). Clearly their international lobbying strategy was achieving results both in terms of access and policy changes.

But then something went wrong – something that the company was completely unprepared for. Genetically modified food and even the company name was sucked into the public debate and suddenly things started to unravel. The corporate strategy had been to ruthlessly target the international locations of political power for a decade or more. It was fine while it lasted but increasingly unpredictable swings of public opinion hit the company hard.

Suddenly the Prime Minister was a more circumspect exponent of GMOs faced with consumer and corporate boycotts of 'Frankenstein foods.' Whatever the rights or wrongs of the case, a

The contagious campaign • part 2

swell of public anger and emotion was heading both for the corporate and political gates.

Monsanto followed a strategy not too dissimilar to Shell's in response (albeit in a much less open and thorough fashion). It set up a web-site which seemed quite open and even featured a link to the Greenpeace web pages criticising the company. However, in order to get to the link, the viewer had to sit through a sequence of 'information' about Monsanto which can only be described as corporate propaganda. It is all well and good linking to your opponent's site but no visitor will arrive there if they have to first sit through an advert that they are paying to watch. Monsanto was facing crisis but still couldn't let go of the control which they had enjoyed over the issue of GMOs. It was seen as spin without substance – a 'Greenwash.'

Just like the cases of Shell and Esso before it, the case of Monsanto demonstrates clearly and unambiguously that if you fail to meet the public's stringent requirements of transparency you are taking a severe business risk. Most companies who try this strategy get away with it most of the time. However, when faced with campaigning organisations such as Greenpeace who thoroughly understand the communications environment in which they are operating, it is like running a heavy machinery depot without any employer's insurance. It's an accident waiting to happen. Companies are meticulous about assessing every other risk but why not the risk that perceptions about their corporate practices could severely damage them in the eyes of the consumer. What do they really have to lose by sharpening up their act?

8.4 • Protecting your image in the era of new media

➡ Consumption is not the new politics as some modern writers seem to suppose. However, the expansion of new media space and the expressive nature of personal consumption have meant that the act of buying has value meaning for a significant portion of the population. This is true of young consumers in particular.

Material need, cultural identity and political action are no longer separated in the way in which they were in the industrial age. New media space invades politics and culture, and in reverse this opens the floodgates for new forms of expression in the market place. Individuals no longer express themselves only through gender, ethnicity, locality and class but through consumption patterns as well. It is a world of self-invention.

Just as it has been seen that politics is having intense difficulty adapting to the era of new media, so are most businesses. They probably have more of an appreciation of the new environment than politicians but it is a fearsome prospect which in itself retards action. Businesses can no longer only appeal to value or lifestyle, they now have to adapt to life meaning also. It is a volatile environment where corporate issues, can suddenly be sucked into the public domain through consumers interacting with NGOs. If you are not ready, you are in severe trouble.

The future will belong to businesses who accept that the values embodied by their brand are now shared and cannot be controlled. Control is temporary, shared ownership is forever. The old outlets, contacts and methods are ceasing to be effective. A number of companies have led the way but will others have the courage to follow?

Sources

- Esso, <http://www.esso.com>.
- Klein, Naomi, *No Logo*, (England, Flamingo, 2000).
- Monbiot, George, *Captive State: the corporate takeover of Britain*, (England, Macmillan, 2001).
- MORI, Ethical Consumerism, <http://www.mori.com/polls/2000.coop-csr.htm>, October 2000.
- Scammell, Margaret, *Internet and civic engagement: Age of the citizen-consumer*, <http://jsis.artsci.washington.edu/programs/cwesuw/scammell.htm>, 2000.
- Shell, People, Planet & Profits: A summary of the Shell Report, 2001. <http://www.shell.com/tellshell>.

Notes on contributors

Editors

Anthony Painter
Anthony Painter is Director and co-founder of Urbanity Ltd (www.urbanity.co.uk), a company specialising in communication through new media. He has worked on a number high profile ecampaigns – for the Labour Party in the 2001 General Election, the Frank Dobson Mayoral campaign and the Britain in Europe campaign.

Anthony was involved in technology and politics pre-dotcom hysteria, as a public affairs consultant and magazine columnist. He feels better prepared for the next wave of irrational exuberance.

E-mail: anthony@urbanity.co.uk

Ben Wardle
Ben Wardle began his career in the communication industry as a lobbyist and media relations consultant for the Campaign for Real Ale (which involved far less time down the pub than his friends would suggest). He worked in similar roles in the public and private sectors before co-founding Urbanity with Anthony Painter.

He built his first website in 1995, but keeps his 'anorak' in a locked drawer for technical emergencies. He's worked on projects for organisations from the Labour Party to the NUJ. Ben is an internet realist who thinks some new technologies have much to offer governments, companies and consumer citizens, but that many technical advances are for geeks only.

E-mail: ben@urbanity.co.uk

Contributors Biographies

Mike Bloxham

Mike Bloxham is recognised as one of the leading figures in digital research.

He founded Netpoll in 1997 to provide clients with the means to assess the effectiveness of their digital communications. The company is now the leading European specialist in user attitudes towards the Internet, mobile devices and Interactive TV.

Mike Bloxham has over ten years experience in market research and in advising major companies on a range of communication issues. He is an expert in concept development, interface testing, site user profiling, user satisfaction surveys and attitudinal research in Europe. This breadth of experience gives him a unique insight into how consumers' attitudes towards interactive platforms continue to evolve and how this impacts on marketing and business strategies.

Andy Mayer

Andy Mayer is senior strategist at Netpoll Ltd, Europe's leading digital research agency. Prior to Netpoll he has worked in both consultancy and the political sector for, amongst others, Accenture, the Pro-Euro Conservative Party, European Movement, P&G, M&S and the *Daily Telegraph*.

In 1999 Andy Mayer ran the UK's first political viral e-mail campaign for Britain in Europe and the first virtual campaigns unit for the PECP European election campaign. He currently directs activities for two digital campaigning organisations, the Euro Information Network and Yes-campaign.com.

Stephan Shakespeare

Stephan Shakespeare was a headmaster in Los Angeles and teacher in a Lambeth comprehensive. He has written extensively on education issues for the national press and ran the Archer London Mayoral Campaign. He founded YouGov in June 2000.

Chris Casey

Chris Casey is the founder of casey.com (formerly CaseyDorin Internet Productions) where he works to help candidates and office holders make the most of the Internet. In the 2000 elections he worked for Hillary Clinton's New York Senate Campaign, Ted Kennedy's Massachusetts re-election campaign, The Democratic Convention in Los Angeles and others.

Previously, Chris worked in the United States Senate for eight years, helping to bring Congress into the Information Age. He also helped bring Kennedy's 1994 Campaign onto the internet, and was a member of the web team at the 1996 Democratic National Convention.

Chris is the creator of CapWeb, a popular online guide to the U.S. Congress, and the author of the book, *The Hill on the Net: Congress Enters the Information Age* (AP Professional, 1996).

E-mail: chris@casey.com

Website: http://www.casey.com

Kate McCarthy

Kate McCarthy is the Labour Party's e-campaign manager. Before working with the Labour Party, she was the Field and Political Director for Choice USA/Voters for Choice, pro-choice organisations based in Washington, DC, USA.

Andrew Saxton

Andrew Saxton is the Labour Party's website editor. He is responsible for the site's content and has extensive experience on newspapers and magazines. He created and launched Labour's first website in 1999. He is responsible for the site's content and believes that typographical errors should be reserved exclusively for the pages of broadsheet newspapers.

Justin Jackson

Justin Jackson is Chief Executive of Politico's Design. He spent six years in the Conservative Research Department, including eighteen months as project manager of conservatives.com. Before that, Justin held a Lectureship in Politics at Brasenose College, Oxford and studied at Nuffield College.